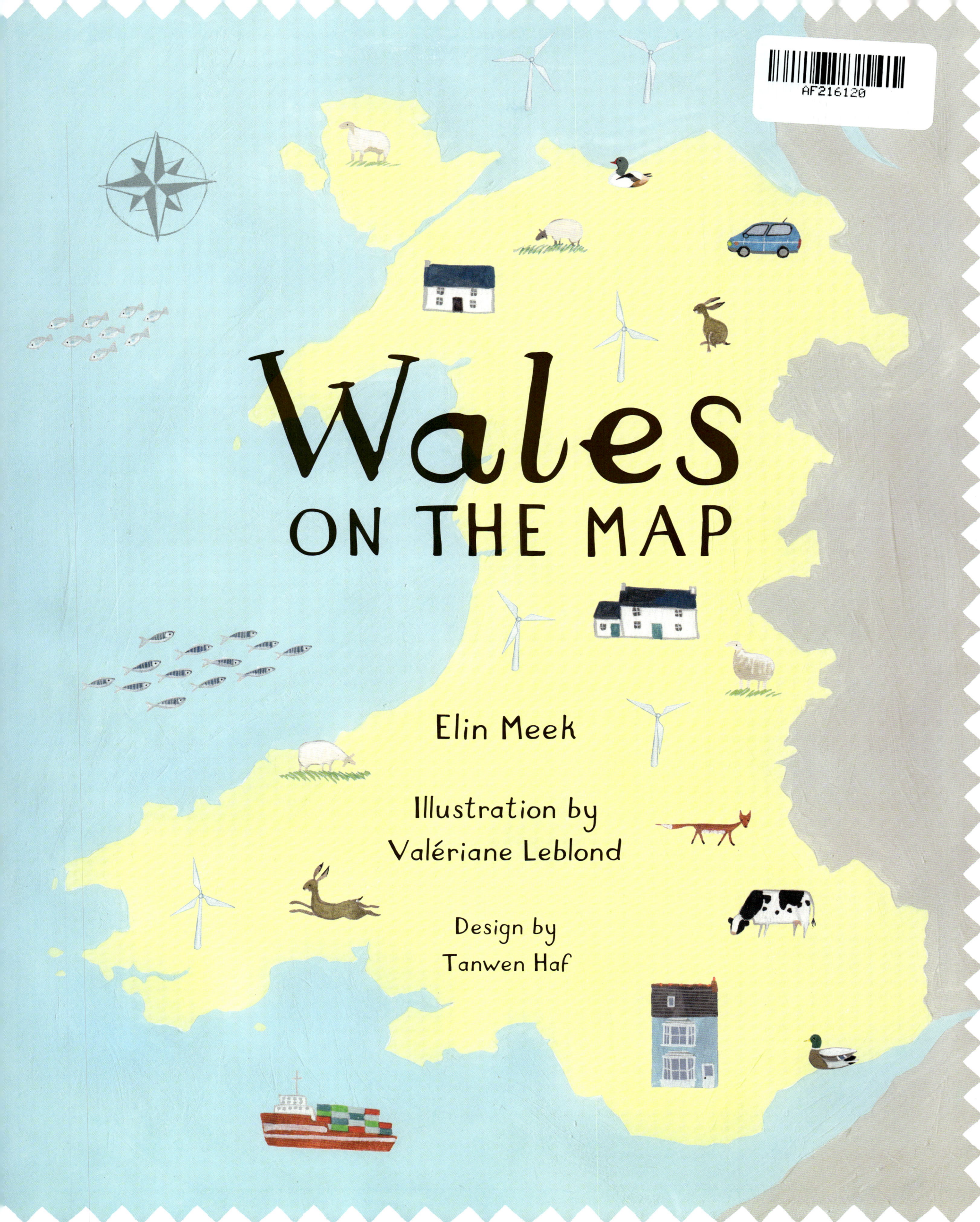

Wales
ON THE MAP

Elin Meek

Illustration by
Valériane Leblond

Design by
Tanwen Haf

To Matthew, who brought me to Wales,
and to Wyre, Alban and Nebo.
Wales — the land of my sons
— Valériane Leblond

Wales was the 'Land of my Mother', and this book
is dedicated to the exquisite, encouraging and exceptional
Mairwen Thomas and to all of our wonderful mothers.
— LT, Rily

Wales
ON THE MAP

Third Edition Reprint 2026 by Dragon Press,
an Imprint of Rily Publications Ltd

First published by Rily Publications Ltd 2018
Rily Publications Ltd, PO Box 257, Caerphilly CF83 9FL
© Rily Publications Ltd 2018

ISBN 978-1-84967-055-5

Text © Elin Meek, 2018
Illustrations © Valériane Leblond, 2018

Fonts designed by Valériane Leblond and Tanwen Haf.

Published with the financial support of the Welsh Books Council.

Printed in China.

dragonpress.co.uk

CONTENTS

ANGLESEY
4–5

CONWY
10–11

FLINTSHIRE
14–15

GWYNEDD
(ARFON AND DWYFOR)
6–7

DENBIGHSHIRE
12–13

WREXHAM
16–17

GWYNEDD
(MEIRIONNYDD)
8–9

POWYS
(MONTGOMERYSHIRE)
20–21

CEREDIGION
18–19

POWYS
(OLD RADNORSHIRE AND BRECONSHIRE)
22–23

TORFAEN
45

PEMBROKESHIRE
24–25

CARMARTHENSHIRE
26–27

MERTHYR TYDFIL
38–39

BLAENAU GWENT
44

MONMOUTHSHIRE
48–49

NEATH PORT TALBOT
30–31

CAERPHILLY
42–43

SWANSEA
28–29

RHONDDA CYNON TAFF
36–37

CARDIFF
40–41

BRIDGEND
32–33

VALE OF GLAMORGAN
34–35

NEWPORT
46–47

FACTS

Forestry covers 13% of the land.

Grass and grazing land comprise 74% of the land.

Crops are grown on 3% of the land.

10% of Wales's land is in urban areas.

IMPORTANT DATES

1 JANUARY — New Year's Day	**13 JANUARY** — Old New Year's Day, celebrated in Pembrokeshire	**25 JANUARY** — St Dwynwen's Day, the Welsh patron saint of lovers	**1 MARCH** — St David's Day
MAY — The Urdd Eisteddfod	**JULY** — The Royal Welsh Agricultural Show	**AUGUST** — The National Eisteddfod of Wales	**16 SEPTEMBER** — Owain Glyndŵr Day
15 OCTOBER — Shwmae Sumae Day – day to greet people in Welsh	**31 OCTOBER** — Halloween	**11 DECEMBER** — Llywelyn ap Gruffudd's Day (last Welsh Prince of Wales)	**25 DECEMBER** — Christmas Day

Shwmae   Sumae

Bala Lake (Llyn Tegid) is the largest natural lake in Wales. It's four miles long and a mile wide.

Pistyll Rhaeadr is Wales's highest waterfall. Water falls for 80 metres. That's higher than Niagara Falls!

· The river Severn (220 miles) is the longest river which rises in Wales, but it also flows through England.

Wales's National Parks
There are three national parks in Wales since:

1951 — Eryri (Snowdonia)

1952 — Pembrokeshire Coast Park

The parks make up 20% of the whole area of Wales.

1956 — The Gower Peninsula became the first place in Britain to be designated as an Area of Outstanding Natural Beauty.

1957 — Bannau Brycheiniog (Brecon Beacons)

−23.3°C was the lowest temperature recorded in Wales, in Rhayader, Powys, in 1940.

37.1°C was the highest temperature recorded in Wales, in Hawarden, Flintshire, in 2022.

· West Wales gets 40% more rain than east Wales.
· Crib Goch mountain, Gwynedd, holds the record for the highest monthly rainfall in Britain — 1396.4mm in December 2015.

Wales is one of the wettest countries in Europe.

National costume worn on St David's Day

· black hat
· betgwn
· apron
· shawl

· Wales rugby shirt
· flat cap

Wales has more castles per square mile than any other country — there used to be around 600, with 100 still standing!

CYMRU AM BYTH!

Motto
"Cymru am Byth!"
(Wales for ever)

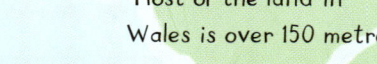

Most of the land in
Wales is over 150 metres.

Yr Wyddfa (Snowdon) (1,085m) is
the highest mountain in Wales.

There are around 160 miles
from the north to the south.

There are between 60 miles and
124 miles from the east to the west.

· 71% of the Welsh population live in urban areas.
· 20% of the Welsh population live in villages
where fewer than 1,500 people live.

The area
of Wales is
8,000 square
miles.

Transport
· The first roads in Wales were built by the Romans.
· The Welsh Government looks after the M4 motorway,
which is 75 miles long, and 1,000 miles of other main
roads. The local councils look after the rest.
· The first railways were built to transport
coal to the ports.
· The railway in Wales often follows
the coast, in order to avoid
the mountains.

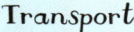

The Welsh language
· 17.8% of the population of Wales
say that they can speak Welsh.
The highest percentage (64.4%) is in
Gwynedd, and the lowest percentage
(6.2%) is in Blaenau Gwent.
· 23% of Welsh pupils go to
Welsh-medium schools.
· Radio Cymru, the Welsh-language
radio station, was established in 1977.
· S4C, the Welsh-language television
channel, was established in 1982.

Around 5,000 people
speak Welsh in Patagonia,
Argentina, where Welsh settlers
went to live in the 19th century.

You can walk the Wales Coast Path which is 870 miles long.

The coastline of Wales is 1,370 miles long.

The official languages of Wales are

Welsh and English.

The highest percentage of people over
65 years old (27.8%) is in Powys.

There are 7 cities in Wales
1. Cardiff was made capital of Wales in 1955.
2. St Davids in Pembrokeshire is the smallest city
in Britain. Less than 2,000 people live there.
3. St Asaph has nearly 3,500 residents.
4. Swansea was made a city in 1969. Although it
is the only city in Wales without a cathedral,
it has had Wales's first minster since 2025.
5. Bangor has been a city since the 6th century.
6. Newport was made a city in 2002. Newport's
history dates back to a Celtic settlement
2000 years ago. The city's location at the mouth
of the River Usk has attracted visitors for centuries.
7. Wrexham is Wales's newest city and it was granted
that status in 2022. It is home to Wrexham A.F.C.
(one of the oldest professional football teams in the world)!

There are 4 UNESCO
World Heritage Sites in
Wales and 1 UNESCO City
of Literature. Can you
find them in this book?

· Over 3.1 million people live in
Wales (3,164,000 in 2023)
· 75% of the Welsh population
live in south-east Wales.

Government
· Wales has had a National Assembly since 1998.
· The Assembly's home is in the Senedd building in
Cardiff Bay.
· From May 2026, there will be 96 Assembly Members.

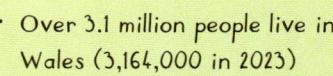

The highest percentage
of children between 0
and 4 years old (15.23%)
is in Newport.

ANGLESEY

714 km² (276 miles²)

Rugby player George North was brought up on Anglesey.

Llynnon Mill (1775) is the only working windmill in Wales.

CEMAES BAY

LLYN ALAW

North Stack

South Stack Lighthouse

A great place to see seabirds, after going down 400 steps!

Holyhead

Ferries sail from this port to Dublin and Dún Laoghaire in Ireland.

HOLY ISLAND

Llanddeusant

Anglesey used to produce enough grain to feed the whole of Wales, so it was called 'Môn, Mother of Wales'.

RIVER ALAW

TREARDDUR BAY

There are about 1,200 shipwrecks around the island for divers to explore.

to Cardiff

Osian Roberts, who used to be one of the Wales football team coaches, was brought up in Bodffordd.

Anglesey Sea Zoo is the largest aquarium in Wales.

The ruins of Llys Rhosyr, one of Llywelyn ab Iorwerth's courts in the 13th century, can be seen here.

The ruins of the Church of Saint Dwynwen, the Welsh patron saint of lovers, is on the island.

Llanddwyn Island

THE ANGLESEY COASTAL PATH IS 125 MILES (200KM) LONG.

Amlwch

Copper was mined on Parys Mountain for centuries. Today the landscape is red like Mars, with moon-like craters.

Moelfre RNLI lifeboatman Richard Evans (1905–2001) is commemorated by a statue. He is one of only 5 people who have been awarded the RNLI gold medal, for saving 281 lives.

Moelfre

MYNYDD BODAFON

Near Moelfre, the *Royal Charter* was shipwrecked, one of the worst shipwrecks in Britain in the 19th century. 452 people drowned.

Puffin Island

RED WHARF BAY

LLYN CEFNI

Works by the Anglesey artists Sir Kyffin Williams and Charles Tunnicliffe can be seen in Oriel Ynys Môn.

Bodffordd

Llangefni

Beaumaris castle (1295) is Edward I's last and strongest castle in Wales. It's a World Heritage Site.

LLANFAIRPWLLGWYNGYLLGOGERYCHWYRNDROBWLLLLANTYSILIOGOGOGOCH

Beaumaris ★
■ CASTLE

This is the longest place name in Europe, but Llanfair PG is the short version!

Llanfairpwllgwyngyll gogerychwyrndrobwll llantysiliogogogoch

RIVER CEFNI

Thomas Telford's **Menai Bridge** (1826) is 417m long. Before the bridge was built, a ferry crossed the Menai Strait.

Menai Bridge

Britannia Bridge

Brynsiencyn

MENAI STRAIT

There are four limestone lions, a pair either end of Robert Stephenson's **Britannia Bridge** (1850).

GWYNEDD

Newborough

Pili Palas is home to butterflies, insects, and other creatures.

GWYNEDD

2,548 km² (984 miles²)

ARFON AND DWYFOR

Many people say that Caernarfon is the most Welsh town in Wales.

Edward I's castle (1296) is a World Heritage Site.

Sain, the first Welsh independent recording company, has a recording studio in Llandwrog. The singer Dafydd Iwan was one of the founders in 1969.

ARFON
POPULATION ABOUT
61,700

DWYFOR
POPULATION ABOUT
27,000

Granite from Trefor quarry is used to make curling stones.

CAERNARFON BAY

Trefor

Nant Gwrtheyrn

An old granite quarry village, which is now a centre for learning Welsh.

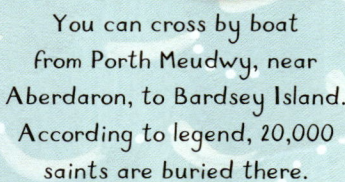

You can cross by boat from Porth Meudwy, near Aberdaron, to Bardsey Island. According to legend, 20,000 saints are buried there.

David Lloyd George, the British Prime Minister between 1916 and 1922, lived here. His statue can be seen on the Maes in the centre of Caernarfon.

Llanystumdwy

WALES COAST PATH

LLŶN PENINSULA

Plas Heli is home to the National Sailing Academy.

Pwllheli

Aberdaron

Aber-soch

BARDSEY ISLAND

A popular seaside resort.

ST TUDWAL'S ISLAND WEST

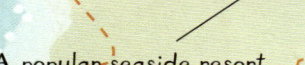

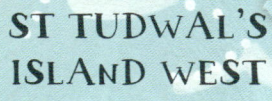

Saint Deiniol established a monastery at Bangor in the 6th century. It has a cathedral and a university.

Bangor

The Romans established their Segontium fort here around AD 78.

Port Dinorwic

Slate from the Dinorwig Slate Quarry used to be exported from here in the 19th century. There is a marina here today.

Bethesda

Caernarfon
CASTLE

ARFON

CARNEDD LLYWELYN

An important village in the slate quarrying area. Today you can fly on a zip wire in the old Penrhyn Quarry, where there is a statue called 'Celebrating Blue Slate'.

The highest peak in Wales at 1,085m. Many paths lead to the summit, or you can take the mountain railway from Llanberis.

Llanberis

DOLBADARN CASTLE

The Slate Landscape of Northwest Wales was designated a UNESCO World Heritage Site in July 2021.

Llandwrog

GLYDER FAWR

Llywelyn ab Iorwerth built the castle around 1230.

YR WYDDFA (SNOWDON)

The National Slate Museum is at Llanberis.

ERYRI

DWYFOR

The Snowdon Lily grows in Eryri (Snowdonia), the area of the highest mountains in Wales. This is the only place in Britain where it grows.

Beddgelert

You can go underground to see the historic Sygun copper mine.

Blaenau Ffestiniog

RIVER GLASLYN

Cricieth
CASTLE

Porthmadog

RIVER DWYRYD

MEIRIONNYDD

TREMADOG BAY

One of Llywelyn ab Iorwerth's castles (1230s).

ERYRI NATIONAL PARK

Ffestiniog slate used to be exported from Porthmadog. You can travel by steam train from here to Blaenau Ffestiniog or to Caernarfon.

CONWY

GLESL

GWYNEDD
POPULATION ABOUT
117,400
★ ★ ★

MEIRIONNYDD
POPULATION ABOUT
28,700

DWYFOR

Portmeirion

RIVER DWYRYD

Maentwrog

MOELWYN MAWR

An Italian-style village, built between 1925 and 1976 by the architect Clough Williams-Ellis.

Plas Tan y Bwlch was home to the Oakeley family, owners of the slate quarries in Blaenau Ffestiniog.

LLYN TRAWSFYNYDD

Trawsfynydd

Harlech
CASTLE

One of Edward I's castles (1289) which is a World Heritage Site. Owain Glyndŵr gained control of the castle in 1404 and held his second parliament here in 1405.

RHINOG FAWR

RHINOG FACH

COED-Y-BRENIN

ERYRI NATIONAL

Hedd Wyn, from 'Yr Ysgwrn' farm, Trawsfynydd, was killed in a battle at the end of the First World War, before he knew that he had won the chair in the National Eisteddfod.

CARDIGAN BAY

Barmouth

RIVER MAWDDACH

An important port for exporting wool, slate and lead in the 18th and 19th centuries. Today it's a seaside resort.

Llywelyn ab Iorwerth started work on the castle around 1221.

Dolgellau

CADAIR IDRIS

WALES COAST PATH

CASTELL Y BERE

Llanfihangel-y-Pennant

The author Manon Steffan Ros lives in the Tywyn area.

RIVER DYSYNNI

There is a memorial here to Mary Jones, who walked around 28 miles (45km) to Bala in 1800 when she was 15, to buy a Bible from Thomas Charles.

You can travel on the Tal-y-llyn railway from Tywyn to Nant Gwernol.

Tywyn

A busy port where ships were built in the 19th century. Tourists flock here today.

Aberdyfi

RIVER DYFI

CEREDIGION

8

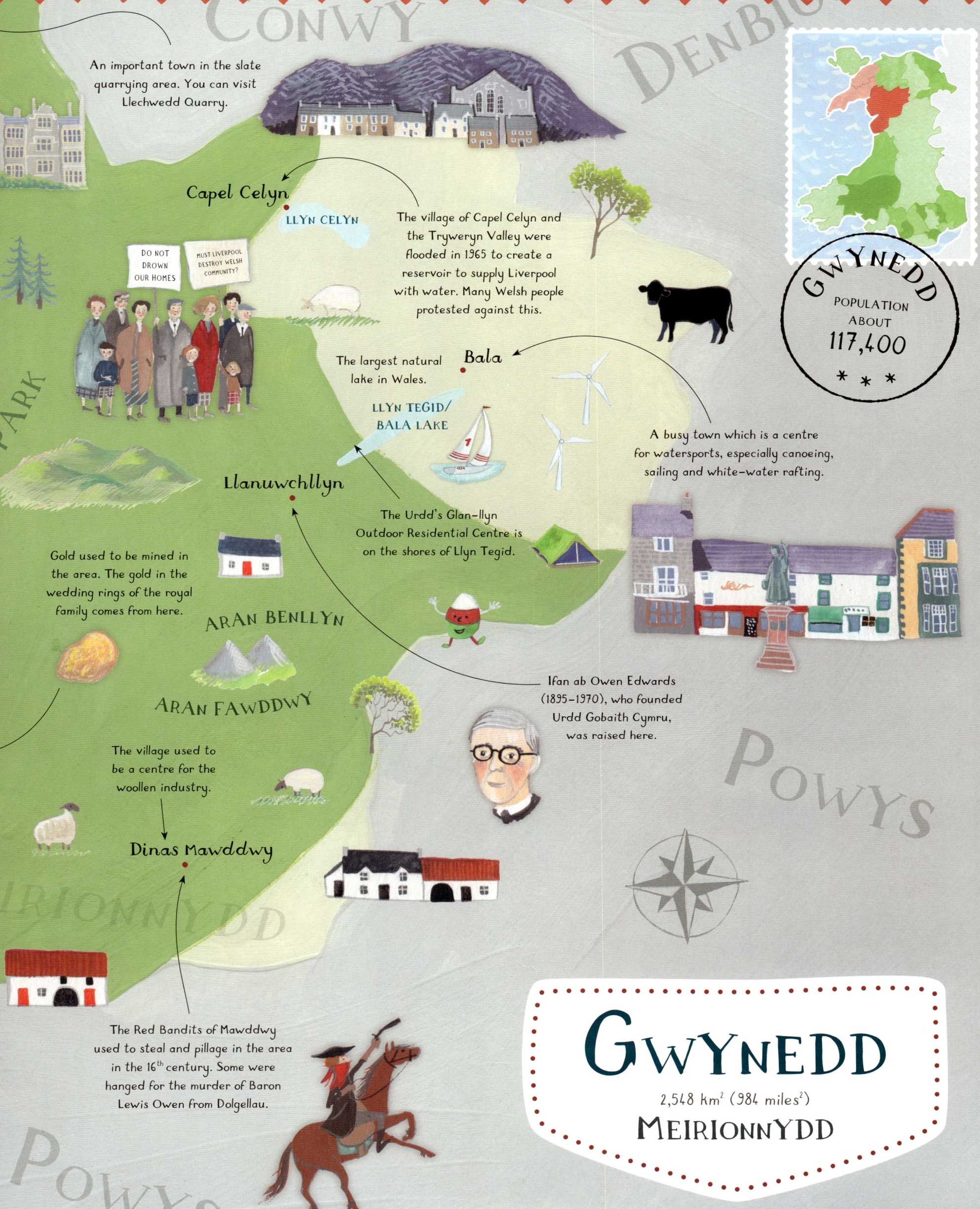

An important town in the slate quarrying area. You can visit Llechwedd Quarry.

Capel Celyn

LLYN CELYN

DO NOT DROWN OUR HOMES

MUST LIVERPOOL DESTROY WELSH COMMUNITY?

The village of Capel Celyn and the Tryweryn Valley were flooded in 1965 to create a reservoir to supply Liverpool with water. Many Welsh people protested against this.

The largest natural lake in Wales.

Bala

LLYN TEGID/ BALA LAKE

A busy town which is a centre for watersports, especially canoeing, sailing and white-water rafting.

Llanuwchllyn

The Urdd's Glan-llyn Outdoor Residential Centre is on the shores of Llyn Tegid.

Gold used to be mined in the area. The gold in the wedding rings of the royal family comes from here.

ARAN BENLLYN

ARAN FAWDDWY

Ifan ab Owen Edwards (1895–1970), who founded Urdd Gobaith Cymru, was raised here.

The village used to be a centre for the woollen industry.

Dinas Mawddwy

The Red Bandits of Mawddwy used to steal and pillage in the area in the 16th century. Some were hanged for the murder of Baron Lewis Owen from Dolgellau.

CONWY

DENBIG

PARK

IRIONNYDD

POWYS

POWYS

GWYNEDD

POPULATION ABOUT 117,400

★ ★ ★

GWYNEDD

2,548 km² (984 miles²)

MEIRIONNYDD

Tourists love to walk along the promenade at Llandudno.

You can reach the summit of the Great Orme by foot, by car, tram or cable car.

It is said that the smallest house in Britain is on the quay in Conwy.

ANGLESEY

Llandudno

DEGANWY CASTLE

Colwyn Bay

CASTLE Conwy

Penmaen-mawr

Llandudno Junction

Conwy castle was built by Edward I and completed in 1287. It's a UNESCO World Heritage Site.

Conwy is famous for its 19th century bridges – Thomas Telford's Suspension Bridge and Robert Stephenson's tubular rail bridge.

Conwy is one of the finest medieval walled towns in Britain.

Bodnant Garden

The RSPB reserve on the banks of the river Conwy is a great place to see all kinds of birds, whatever the season.

VALE OF CONWY

GWYNEDD

Trefriw

LLYN CRAFNANT

Llanrwst

ERYRI NATIONAL PARK

Capel Curig

Betws-y-coed

Plas y Brenin is the National Mountain Centre.

MOEL SIABOD

Visitors have been coming here since Victorian times to see the Swallow Falls.

Dolwyddelan

CASTLE

Dolwyddelan castle is one of the princes of Gwynedd's castles. Llywelyn ab Iorwerth (Llywelyn the Great) is said to have been born here in 1173.

RIVER CONWY

LLYWELYN AB IORWERTH

10

WALES COAST PATH

Towyn

Abergele

All kinds of wild animals can be seen in the Welsh Mountain Zoo.

Extensive flooding occurred in Towyn in 1990. Thousands of people had to be evacuated. The sea defences have been improved since then.

Llanfair Talhaiarn

DENBIGHSHIRE

FLINTSHIRE

Llansannan

You can see Welsh woollen products being made at Trefriw woollen mills.

There is an arch bridge in Llanrwst dating back to the 17th century. A driver at one end can't see a vehicle at the other end.

The worst railway accident in Wales happened here in 1868. 33 people were killed.

Tourists flock to Conwy's coast in the summer.

LLYN BRENIG

LLYN ALWEN

Pentrefoelas

Do you think the Ugly House is ugly?

Cerrigydrudion

Stagecoach horses used to be changed here, on the A5 between London and Holyhead. The road was built by Thomas Telford. Some passengers sailed on to Ireland from Holyhead.

CONWY
1,130 km² (440 miles²)

NEDD

DENBIGHSHIRE

ENGLAND

INTSHIRE

CLWYDIAN RANGE

RIVER DEE

DENBIGHSHIRE

POPULATION ABOUT 95,800

One of the first holiday camps was situated here.

Prestatyn became a fashionable seaside resort after the railway came in 1848.

Rhuddlan castle is one of Edward I's castles in Wales. The building work began in 1277.

You can walk along some of the most complete medieval town walls in Britain.

There was a mental asylum here from 1848 to 1995.

• Llandyrnog

CASTLE • Prestatyn

WALES COAST PATH

Marine Lake is the only saltwater lake in north Wales. You can ride on the oldest miniature railway in Britain here.

CASTLE • Denbigh

Rhyl Air Show is held over the August Bank Holiday weekend.

Rhyl •

CASTLE • Rhuddlan
• Bodelwyddan
• St Asaph

Ysgol Glan Clwyd is the oldest Welsh-medium comprehensive school in Wales. It opened in Rhyl in 1956 before moving to St Asaph in 1969.

People have been coming to Rhyl for centuries to enjoy the beach, the sea and the promenade.

A city of around 4,000 people. The ancient cathedral here is the smallest in Britain. Its greatest treasure is an original copy of William Morgan's Welsh Bible from the 16th century.

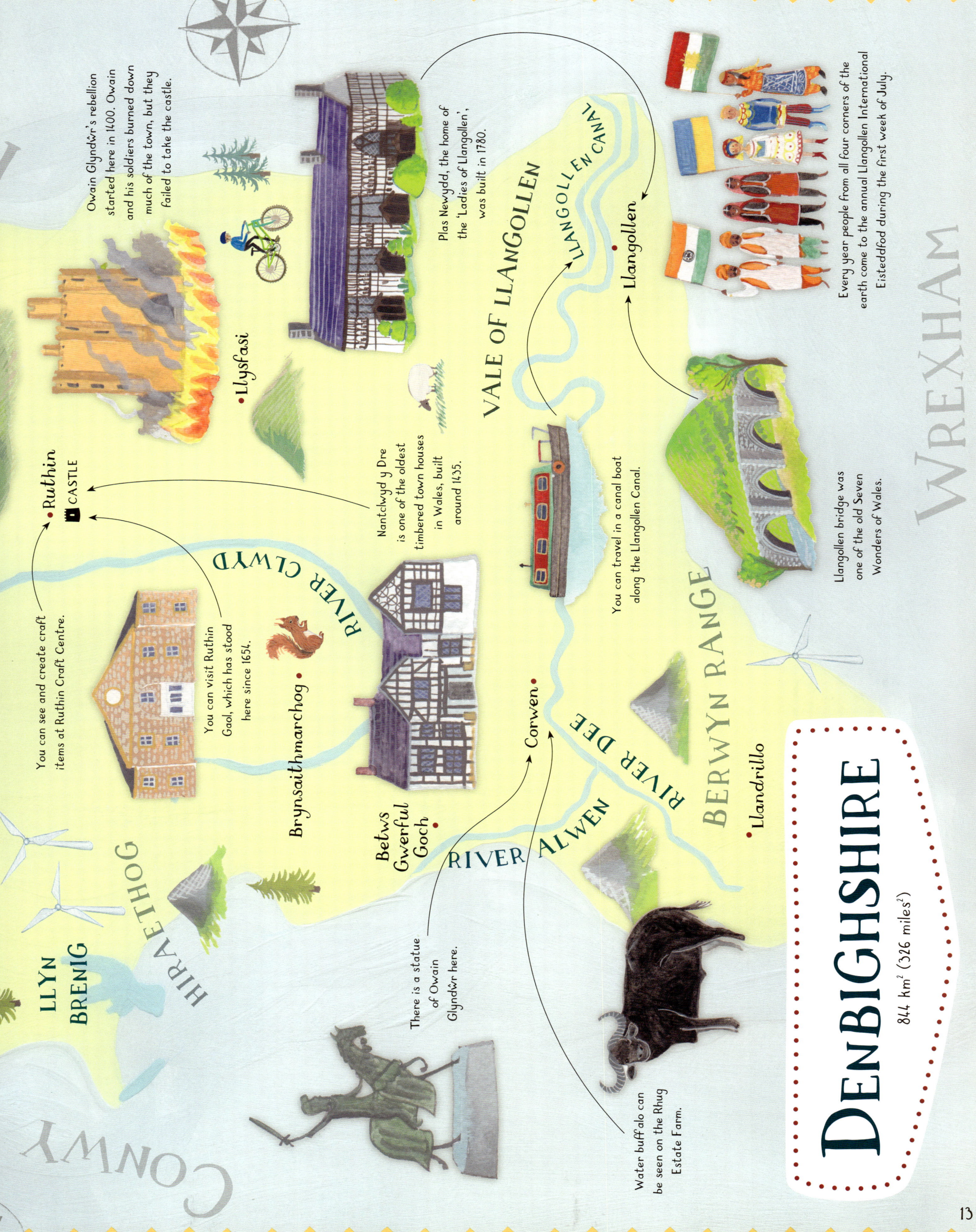

Owain Glyndŵr's rebellion started here in 1400. Owain and his soldiers burned down much of the town, but they failed to take the castle.

Plas Newydd, the home of the 'Ladies of Llangollen', was built in 1780.

Every year people from all four corners of the earth come to the annual Llangollen International Eisteddfod during the first week of July.

VALE OF LLANGOLLEN

LLANGOLLEN CANAL

•Llangollen

•Llysfasi

Nantclwyd y Dre is one of the oldest timbered town houses in Wales, built around 1435.

•Ruthin ■ CASTLE

You can travel in a canal boat along the Llangollen Canal.

Llangollen bridge was one of the old Seven Wonders of Wales.

You can see and create craft items at Ruthin Craft Centre.

You can visit Ruthin Gaol, which has stood here since 1654.

RIVER CLWYD

Brynsaithmarchog •

Betws Gwerful Goch •

Corwen •

BERWYN RANGE

•Llandrillo

LLYN BRENIG

HIRAETHOG

RIVER ALWEN

RIVER DEE

There is a statue of Owain Glyndŵr here.

Water buffalo can be seen on the Rhug Estate Farm.

DENBIGHSHIRE
844 km² (326 miles²)

FLINTSHIRE

169 km² (438 miles²)

ENGLAND

FLINTSHIRE
POPULATION ABOUT 155,000

Pilgrims have been coming to St Winefride's Well since AD 660. Many people believe the waters have healing powers.

Edward I built a castle here between 1277 and 1285.

The ice rink in the Deeside Leisure Centre is home of the National Centre for Ice Sports in Wales.

THE MOUTH OF THE RIVER DEE

Flint • CASTLE

• Holywell

HALKYN MOUNTAIN

Mostyn •

TALACRE LIGHTHOUSE

Point of Ayr

Site of one of the last deep coal mines in Wales, which closed in 1996.

There has been a port here for over a thousand years. It has been extended in the 21st century, so that large ships can berth here.

WREXHAM

Saltney

Prime Minister William Gladstone lived here in the 19th century.

Queensferry

WALES COAST PATH

Hawarden
✈ There is an airport here.

Broughton

Wings for the Airbus aircraft are built here.

AIRBUS A380

Shotton
There has been a steelworks here since 1896.

Ewloe
CASTLE

A Bronze Age bowl was discovered near the castle in 1823. It has decorations showing waves, oars and shields.

Caergwrle
CASTLE

Ewloe Castle was built by Llywelyn ap Gruffudd in 1257.

Mold
CASTLE

In 1833, a gold cape from the Bronze Age (1900 – 1600 BC) was found here. It is kept in the British Museum in London.

Rhyd-y-mwyn

RIVER ALUN

CLWYDIAN RANGE

MOEL FAMA

There is a statue of Daniel Owen, the first Welsh novelist, here.

DANIEL OWEN

Former industries in Flintshire include lead and coal mining, cotton spinning and producing paper and silk ribbons.

DENBIGHSHIRE

WREXHAM

499 km² (193 miles²)

In 2022, Wrexham became the seventh city in Wales.

In 1934, there was a terrible disaster in the Gresford Colliery. 262 colliers were killed by a gas explosion.

The Stiwt (Institute) is an arts centre which is home to a youth theatre company.

Llŷr Williams, the world-famous pianist, comes from Rhos.

Rhosllannerchrugog

Rhos was originally a mining village.

Ruabon

RIVER DEE

Pontcysyllte Aqueduct is a World Heritage Site. It was built by Thomas Telford and William Jessop. Since 1805, it has transported a canal 39m above the river Dee. You can cross the aqueduct by foot along the towpath, or go by barge boat.

Pontcysyllte Aqueduct

Glyn Ceiriog

RIVER CEIRIOG

Chirk

There used to be slate quarries here.

Llanarmon Dyffryn Ceiriog

The Welsh novelist Islwyn Ffowc Elis was brought up here.

Chirk castle is 700 years old and overlooks the town.

The parish church bells were one of the Seven Wonders of Wales.

RIVER DEE

RIVER ALUN

Gresford

ENGLAND

CASTLE
Holt

Wrexham football club was established in 1864. At the end of the 2024/25 season, it became the first ever football club to win a third straight promotion, from being a non-league club in 2021 to playing in the Championship in the 2025/26 season.

You can learn about science at Techniquest Glyndŵr.

WREXHAM

St Giles Church is one of the old Seven Wonders of Wales. The tower can be seen for miles around.

Erddig

You can visit the house and gardens of Erddig, one of Britain's finest stately homes. It was built between 1684 and 1687.

ENGLAND

Overton-on-Dee

Ruabon was famous for its iron, coal and chemicals. Tiles and bricks are still produced here.

The 21 Overton yew trees were one of the Seven Wonders of Wales.

Hanmer

WYNNSTAY ARMS HOTEL, WREXHAM

It's likely that the Football Association of Wales was established at the Wynnstay hotel here in 1876. But the Wynnstay hotel in Wrexham makes the same claim!

WYNNSTAY ARMS HOTEL, RUABON

CEREDIGION

688 km² (1,783 miles²)

The National Library of Wales is the largest library in Wales, keeping a copy of every book and magazine published in Britain. Important maps, photographs and manuscripts are also kept here.

ABERYSTWYTH CEREDIGION
DINAS LLÊN · CITY OF LITERATURE

Aberystwyth was named Wales' first UNESCO City of Literature in October 2025. Many literary events are held here and it is the first town in Wales to have its own poet.

You can go on a boat trip to see dolphins and porpoises in Cardigan Bay.

You can enjoy honey ice cream in this colourful seaside town.

CARDIGAN BAY

Aberaeron

Llanerchaeron

New Quay

Ships used to be built here in the 19th century. Tourists flock here today.

Cardigan Island •

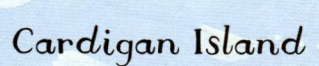

Llangrannog

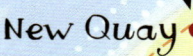

WALES COAST PATH

In the 19th and 20th centuries, it used to be important for ship-building and fishing. There is an airport and meteorological office here today.

Aber-porth

Have you been to the Urdd Gobaith Cymru Camp and Ski Centre here?

Llanerchaeron villa was designed by architect John Nash (1752–1835) around 1794. He went on to design Buckingham Palace and Regent Street, London, and Brighton Pavillion. You can visit the villa and the farm.

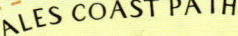

Cardigan
♜ CASTLE

In 1176 Lord Rhys held the first eisteddfod in the castle here. The town used to be an important ship-building centre and port.

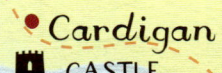

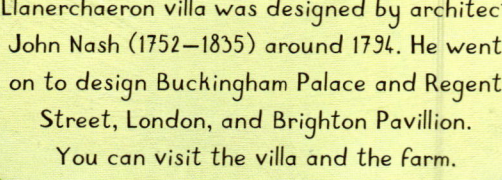

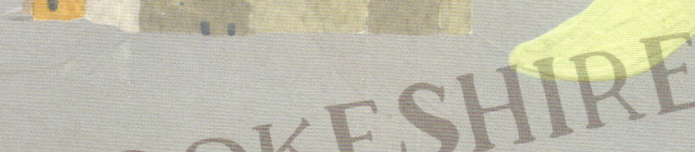

PEMBROKESHIRE

RIVER DYFI

CEREDIGION
POPULATION
ABOUT
71,500
★ ★ ★

PUMLUMON

Hyddgen

The first Welsh university college was established here in 1872.

Steam engines have been pulling carriages along the Vale of Rheidol Railway since 1902.

Owain Glyndŵr won an important battle here on the slopes of Pumlumon in 1401.

CASTLE ▮ • Aberystwyth

RIVER RHEIDOL

RIVER YSTWYTH

STATWS SWYDDOGOL I'R GYMRAEG

On Trefechan Bridge in 1963, the Welsh Language Society held its first protest.

Cwmystwyth •

There used to be many lead and copper mines in this area.

Cors Caron — or Gors Goch Glanteifi — is a National Nature Reserve teeming with wildlife.

Strata Florida

Ceredigion is also known as Cardiganshire.

• Cors Caron
• Tregaron

RIVER AERON

RIVER TEIFI

The 14th century poet Dafydd ap Gwilym is buried in Strata Florida Abbey, although some say that he is at Talley Abbey (Carmarthenshire). The monks copied many important Welsh manuscripts here.

The offices of the Welsh magazine, Golwg are here.

Welsh gold jewellery is made here. Horse trotting races are held here.

CASTLE ▮ • Lampeter

Henry Richard (1812–88), 'The Apostle of Peace', was a Member of Parliament and secretary of the International Peace Society. The local school is named after him.

A small university town which hosts a stallion show every year.

POWYS

2,000 km² (5,179 miles²)

MONTGOMERYSHIRE

Bishop William Morgan translated the Bible into Welsh here in 1588.

Lake Vyrnwy in the Berwyn Mountains was the first reservoir dam in Wales. It was built by Liverpool between 1881 and 1888 to supply the city with water.

LAKE VYRNWY

GWYNEDD

The Centre for Alternative Technology shows how we can live without damaging the earth.

Fashion designer and business woman Laura Ashley opened a clothes factory here in the 1960s; it closed in 2005.

• Machynlleth

Carno •

Owain Glyndŵr held a parliament here in 1404.

CLYWEDOG LAKE

MONTGOMERY

A collection of Welsh quilts can be seen in the Minerva Arts Centre.

Llanidloes •

THE BERWYN MOUNTAINS

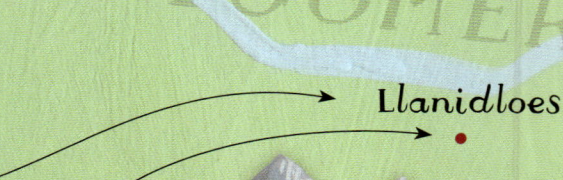

The old Market Hall here (built around 1600) is the only one of its type left in Wales.

CEREDIGION

Pistyll Rhaeadr is Wales's highest waterfall. Water falls over 80 metres. It's one of the Seven Wonders of Wales.

Llanrhaeadr-ym-Mochnant

POWYS
POPULATION ABOUT
133,200
* * *

MONTGOMERYSHIRE
POPULATION ABOUT
64,400

RIVER SEVERN

You can visit the red medieval castle and its lovely gardens.

CASTLE
Welshpool

POWIS CASTLE

Livestock markets are held here.

The Mid Wales Airport is to the south of the town.

Llywelyn ap Gruffudd built the castle in the 1270s.

DOLFORWYN CASTLE

CASTLE
Montgomery

There has been a castle here since the 11th century.

Newtown

The woollen industry was very important in the town in the 19th century.

Pryce Jones started the first mail-order business in the world here in 1861.

There is a museum here to Robert Owen, an industrialist who looked after his workers in New Lanark cotton mills, Scotland, in the 18th century.

There are six dams in the area, built by the city of Birmingham at the end of the 19th and early 20th centuries.

Abbey-cwm-hir

Elan Valley

CLYWEDOG LAKE

Llywelyn ap Gruffudd, the last Welsh prince of Wales (d. 1282), is buried in the abbey.

The World Bog Snorkelling Championship takes place annually every August Bank Holiday near Llanwrtyd Wells.

Llywelyn ap Gruffudd, the last Welsh prince of Wales, was killed here in 1282.

Cilmeri

Llangammarch Wells

Llanwrtyd Wells

Three towns where people came to take the healthy waters.

POWYS

2,000 km² (5,179 miles²)

OLD RADNORSHIRE AND BRECONSHIRE

Frances Hoggan from Brecon was the first woman in Britain and the second woman in Europe to get a degree in medicine.

RIVER USK

EPYNT MOUNTAIN

The Brecon Jazz Festival is very popular every August.

BANNAU BRYCHEINIOG NATIONAL PARK

There is a cathedral here.

Tommy and Jeff Morgan discovered these caves in 1912.

People used to work in the coalmines and the clock-making factory in this area.

Dan-yr-Ogof Caves

Ystradgynlais

Llandrindod is the main town in Powys. In the Victorian era, people used to come here to take the healthy waters.

The National Cycle Museum is here, and a Cycling Festival is held every July.

- Llandrindod Wells

The site of the Royal Welsh Agricultural Show every July, since 1963.

- Llanelwedd
- Builth Wells

RADNORSHIRE
POPULATION ABOUT
25,000

BRECONSHIRE
POPULATION ABOUT
43,800

RIVER WYE

BRONLLYS CASTLE

A motte and bailey castle from the 12th century.

- Brecon

LLANGORSE LAKE

Llangorse Lake is the largest natural lake in south Wales.

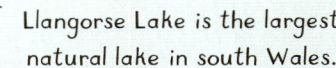

ENGLAND

Pen-y-Fan

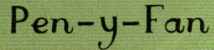
TAL-Y-BONT RESERVOIR

TRETOWER CASTLE

CASTLE
Crickhowell

Sir George Everest (1790–1866) was born here. He was a surveyor who surveyed India. The highest mountain in the world was named after him in 1865. The mountain is called Chomolungma in the Tibetan language.

The highest mountain in south Wales — it's 886m in height.

BLAENAU

MONMOUTHSHIRE

You can travel by ferry from this port to Rosslare in Ireland.

French soldiers landed here in 1797, the last time foreign troops invaded Britain. Local women, led by Jemima Nicholas, captured several soldiers. The French were easily defeated.

Strumble Head

Fishguard

Tregwynt

Gwaun Valley

The woollen products from this famous mill are sold all over the world.

LLYS-Y-FRÂN RESERVOIR

Lime used to be burned in the old kilns when Solva was a busy harbour.

St Davids

The smallest city in Britain. St David's cathedral is here. He is the patron saint of Wales and lived here in the 6th century.

Ramsey Island

Solva

S T   B R I D E S
B A Y

WESTERN CLEDDAU

Pembrokeshire's main town. There has been a castle here since 1110.

Haverfordwest
CASTLE

Puffins and Manx shearwater birds nest here. You can take a boat to see them.

Skomer Island

There is an oil refinery here. The Welsh name means 'mouth of the two Cleddau rivers'.

Milford Haven

Pembroke Dock

PEMBROKE CASTLE

CAREW CASTLE

Henry Tudor landed here in 1485. He travelled to Bosworth, won a battle and was crowned King Henry VII. You could learn to sail here.

Skokholm Island

Dale

Ferries sail from this port to Rosslare in Ireland.

A small church built into a cliff. St Govan lived in a nearby cave in the 6th century.

St Govan's Church

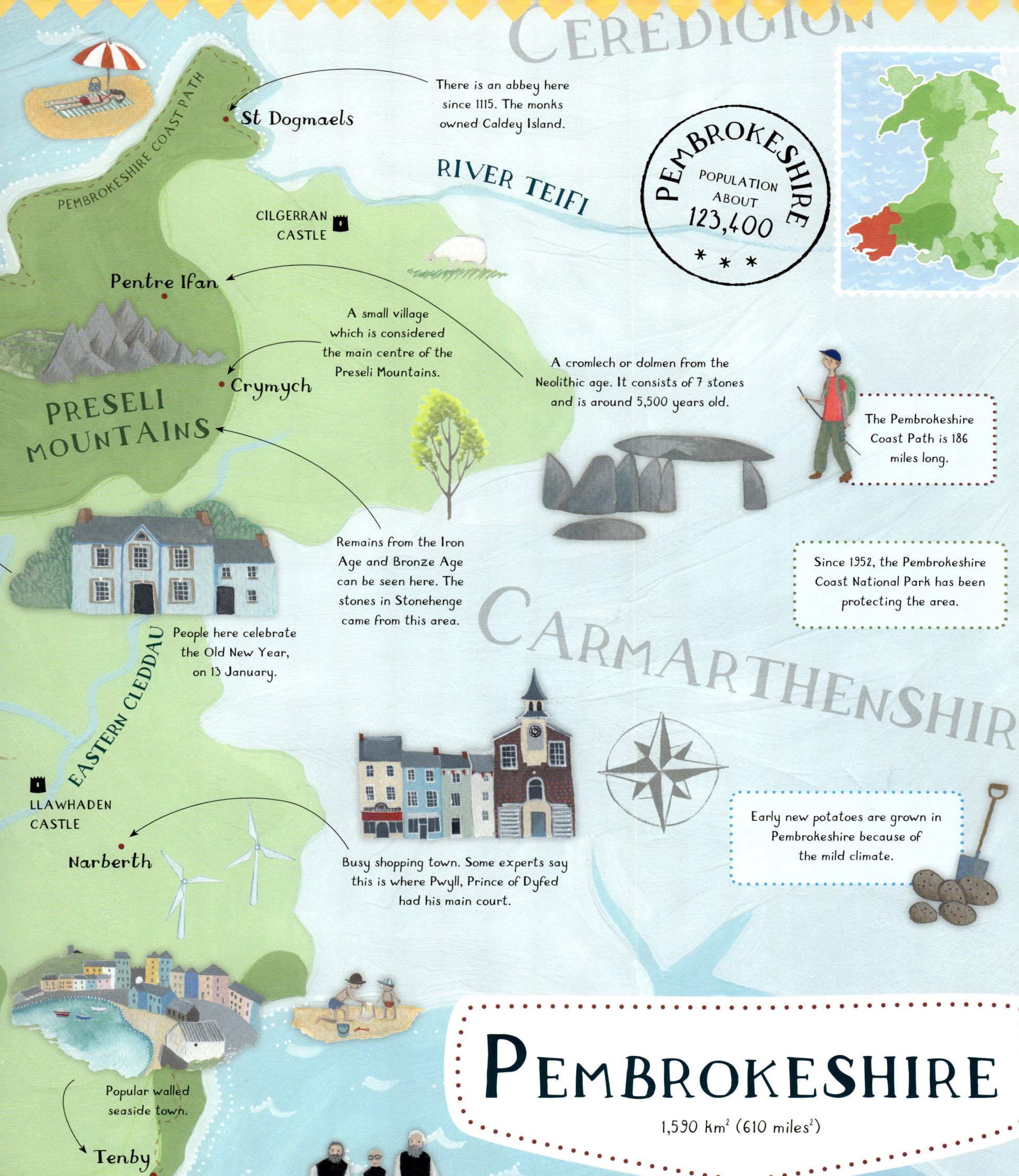

St Dogmaels

There is an abbey here since 1115. The monks owned Caldey Island.

RIVER TEIFI

CILGERRAN CASTLE

PEMBROKESHIRE POPULATION ABOUT 123,400 ★★★

Pentre Ifan

A small village which is considered the main centre of the Preseli Mountains.

A cromlech or dolmen from the Neolithic age. It consists of 7 stones and is around 5,500 years old.

Crymych

The Pembrokeshire Coast Path is 186 miles long.

PRESELI MOUNTAINS

Remains from the Iron Age and Bronze Age can be seen here. The stones in Stonehenge came from this area.

Since 1952, the Pembrokeshire Coast National Park has been protecting the area.

People here celebrate the Old New Year, on 13 January.

CARMARTHENSHIRE

EASTERN CLEDDAU

Early new potatoes are grown in Pembrokeshire because of the mild climate.

LLAWHADEN CASTLE

Narberth

Busy shopping town. Some experts say this is where Pwyll, Prince of Dyfed had his main court.

Popular walled seaside town.

Tenby

PEMBROKESHIRE

1,590 km² (610 miles²)

MANORBIER CASTLE

Caldey Island

Monks live here. They make perfumes and chocolate to sell to tourists.

This is a striking waterfall on the river Teifi. The coracle is used as a fishing boat here.

The National Wool Museum, in the old Cambria woollen mill, tells the story of the woollen industry in this part of the Teifi valley.

Cenarth

CASTLE
Newcastle Emlyn

Llanllwni

Dre-fach Felindre

In 1839, protesters attacked the toll-gate at Efail-wen three times because people had to pay for travelling on turnpike roads. This was the start of the Rebecca Riots. Everyone wore women's clothes so that nobody would recognise them.

There is a memorial outside the Guildhall to remember Gwynfor Evans becoming Plaid Cymru's first MP.

The oldest town in Wales. In the old priory, a monk wrote the Black Book of Carmarthen, the oldest Welsh-language manuscript.

Fishermen use coracles as boats on the river Towy.

PEMBROKESHIRE

Efail-wen

Around AD 940, King Hywel Dda gathered people from all parts of Wales here to organise Welsh laws. There is a Hywel Dda centre and garden here today.

Merlin, the wizard, came from Carmarthen and the story of the old oak tree is linked to him.

Carmarthen
CASTLE

National Botanic Garden of Wales

Whitland

Cockle picking used to be popular here. A ferry used to cross the river Towy to Llansteffan.

RIVER TAF

In 1927, the racing driver John Parry Thomas was killed whilst trying to break the land speed record on the beach in his car, Babs.

Llanddowror

Llansteffan
CASTLE

Llangyndeyrn

GWENDRAETH FACH

Tumble

CASTLE
Laugharne

Ferryside

Pendine

SAVE OUR VALLEY!

CASTLE
Kidwelly

GWENDRAETH FAWR

CARMARTHEN BAY

In 1137, Princess Gwenllian was killed as she led the army of her husband, Gruffudd ap Rhys, against the Normans.

Burry Port

Llanelli

In 1928, Amelia Earhart landed here after flying across the Atlantic. She was the first woman to do so.

Ysgol Gymraeg Llanelli (later Ysgol Dewi Sant) opened in 1947. It was the first Welsh primary school to be opened by a county council.

26

LLYN BRIANNE

Twm Siôn Cati (1530–1610) used to hide in a cave here after stealing from the rich to give to the poor.

The Romans used to mine gold here.

Ystrad-ffin

Dolaucothi Gold Mines

POWYS

You can see the remains of an abbey from 1180 here.

RIVER TOWY
THE LONGEST RIVER IN WALES (68 MILES)

RIVER COTHI

Talley

Llandovery

CASTLE

Drovers used to stop in Llandovery on their way to London to sell the animals they were droving.

William Williams, Pantycelyn, the famous hymn-writer (he wrote 'Bread of Heaven'), comes from this area.

Llyn y Fan Fach
Myddfai

Llandeilo
DINEFWR CASTLE

You can visit Dinefwr Castle, the main court of the princes of Deheubarth in the Middle Ages, and see the rare white cattle.

DRYSLWYN CASTLE

According to legend, a lady came from the lake and married a shepherd. They had sons who became famous physicians (doctors) in the Myddfai area.

Rugby was played for the first time in Wales at Llandovery College around 1850.

CARREG CENNEN CASTLE

There is an enormous Glasshouse here and a Butterfly House.

The main town of the Amman Valley, where coalmining used to be an important industry.

Ammanford

The huge replica of a miner's lamp at the entrance of Mynydd Mawr Woodland Park shows that coalmining used to be an important industry in the Gwendraeth Valley.

NEATH PORT

M4

Between 1959 and 1964, local people campaigned against building a dam in the area, and succeeded!

🚧 M4

CARMARTHENSHIRE

2,395 km^2 (925 miles^2)

Llanelli was famous for tinplate production and the town was called 'Tinopolis'. Today, it's home to the Scarlets regional rugby team.

SWANSEA

CITY AND COUNTY OF SWANSEA

380 km² (150 miles²)

In 1947, 8 Mumbles lifeboat men went out in a storm to try and rescue a group of 39 men on board the *SS Samptampa* near Porthcawl. Every member of the lifeboat team and all the men on board the ship died. There are stained glass windows commemorating this in Oystermouth church.

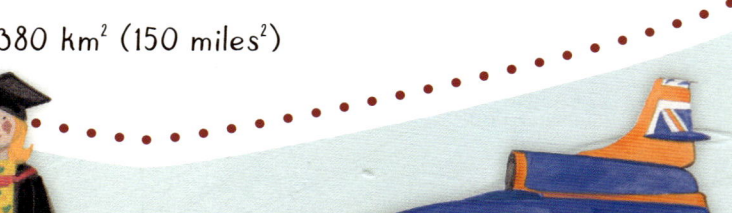

🎓 Swansea University

The Engineering Department at Swansea University have taken part in developing Bloodhound SSC. This is a car which will attempt to travel at 1,000 miles per hour, and break the land speed record.

CARMARTH

The centre of Swansea was destroyed in February 1941, during the Second World War.

Swansea Jack

Swansea Jack was a dog who saved a 12-year-old who had fallen into the docks in the 1930s and even more people, possibly. There is a memorial to him on the promenade. Swansea people are now called Swansea Jacks.

WEOBLEY CASTLE

Dylan Thomas

Dylan Thomas (1914–53), the poet and author, was born and raised in Swansea.

RHOSSILI BAY

• **Llangennith**
A great place for surfing!

The Gower Peninsula is one of the Areas of Outstanding Natural Beauty in Wales

GOWER PENINSULA

One of the most beautiful beaches in Gower.

PENNARD CASTLE

CEFN BRYN

• Worm's Head

• Rhossili

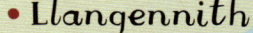

Three Cliff's Bay •

OXWICH BAY

The skeleton of the 'Red lady of Paviland' was found here in 1823. In fact, it was a young man who lived around 24,000 BC.

• Goat's Hole Cave, Paviland

• Port Eynon

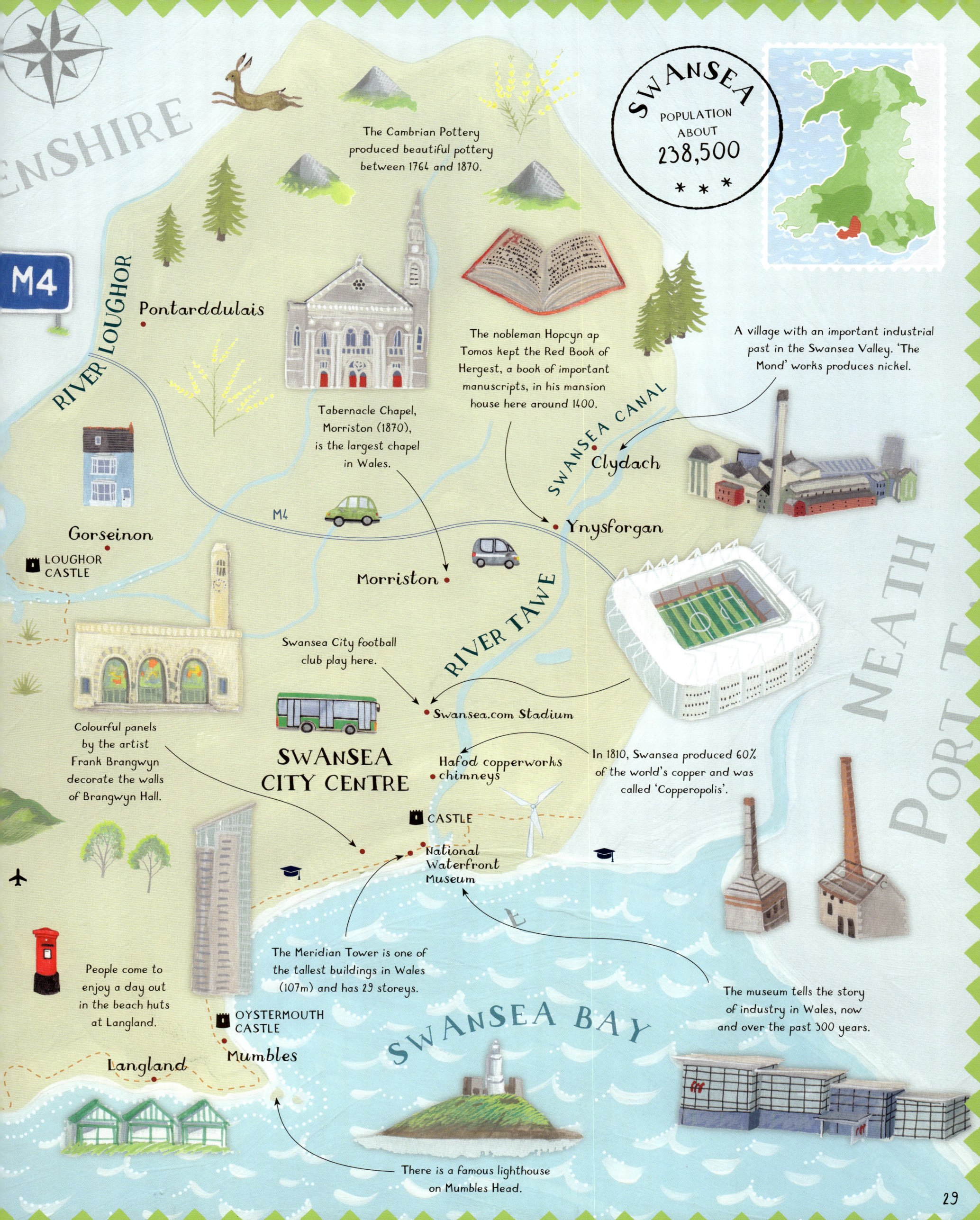

ENSHIRE

M4

RIVER LOUGHOR

Pontarddulais

The Cambrian Pottery produced beautiful pottery between 1764 and 1870.

The nobleman Hopcyn ap Tomos kept the Red Book of Hergest, a book of important manuscripts, in his mansion house here around 1400.

A village with an important industrial past in the Swansea Valley. 'The Mond' works produces nickel.

Tabernacle Chapel, Morriston (1870), is the largest chapel in Wales.

SWANSEA CANAL

Clydach

Gorseinon

LOUGHOR CASTLE

M4

Morriston

Ynysforgan

RIVER TAWE

Swansea City football club play here.

Swansea.com Stadium

Colourful panels by the artist Frank Brangwyn decorate the walls of Brangwyn Hall.

SWANSEA CITY CENTRE

Hafod copperworks chimneys

In 1810, Swansea produced 60% of the world's copper and was called 'Copperopolis'.

CASTLE

National Waterfront Museum

People come to enjoy a day out in the beach huts at Langland.

The Meridian Tower is one of the tallest buildings in Wales (107m) and has 29 storeys.

The museum tells the story of industry in Wales, now and over the past 300 years.

OYSTERMOUTH CASTLE

Mumbles

SWANSEA BAY

NEATH PORT T

Langland

There is a famous lighthouse on Mumbles Head.

29

NEATH PORT TALBOT

442 km² (171 miles²)

POWYS

Pontneathvaughan

Blaengwrach

Resolven

Onllwyn

The grave of Dic Penderyn, or Richard Lewis (1807–31), is in the cemetery of St Mary's Church, Aberavon. When he was a collier in Merthyr, he took part in a riot there and was accused of harming a soldier. He was hanged for this in Cardiff, although he was innocent. His final words were "O Lord, what an injustice (a wrong)!"

Neath Valley is famous for its beautiful waterfalls. You can walk behind Sgwd yr Eira.

NEATH VALLEY

In Cefn Coed Colliery Museum you can learn about the history of the deepest anthracite coalmine in the world at one time.

Crynant

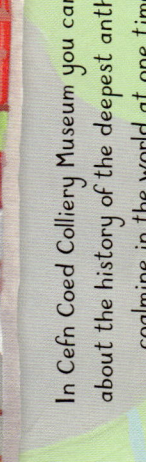

Ystalyfera

Cwmllynfell

You can come here to see the waterfalls and the old tin works.

CARMARTHENSHIRE

The rugby player Gareth Edwards was born in Gwaun-cae-gurwen.

Gwauncaegurwen

There were steelworks and tinplate works here from 1860 to 1962.

Pontardawe

SWANSEA CANAL

RIVER TAWE

SWANSEA

Blaengwynfi

The park is great for cycling and mountain-biking.

Richard Burton, a famous actor in the 20th century, was born here.

Afan Forest Park

The Romans established a fort called Nidum here in AD 70–80.

The Welsh Rugby Union was established in a meeting here in 1881.

Pontrhydyfen

There is a striking aqueduct here.

The actor Sir Anthony Hopkins was born here.

The park includes Margam Castle, the Orangery and the remains of Margam Abbey.

Many deer live in the park.

Margam Country Park

M4

RIVER AFAN

RIVER NEATH

NEATH CANAL

Aberdulais

Neath

Neath Abbey

Briton Ferry

TENNANT CANAL

Old parts of the Abbey (between 1180 and 1330) can still be seen today.

Port Talbot

M4

Aberavon

ABERAVON BEACH

There has been a large steelworks here since 1952, the largest in Europe at one time.

SWANSEA BAY

A popular beach with surfers.

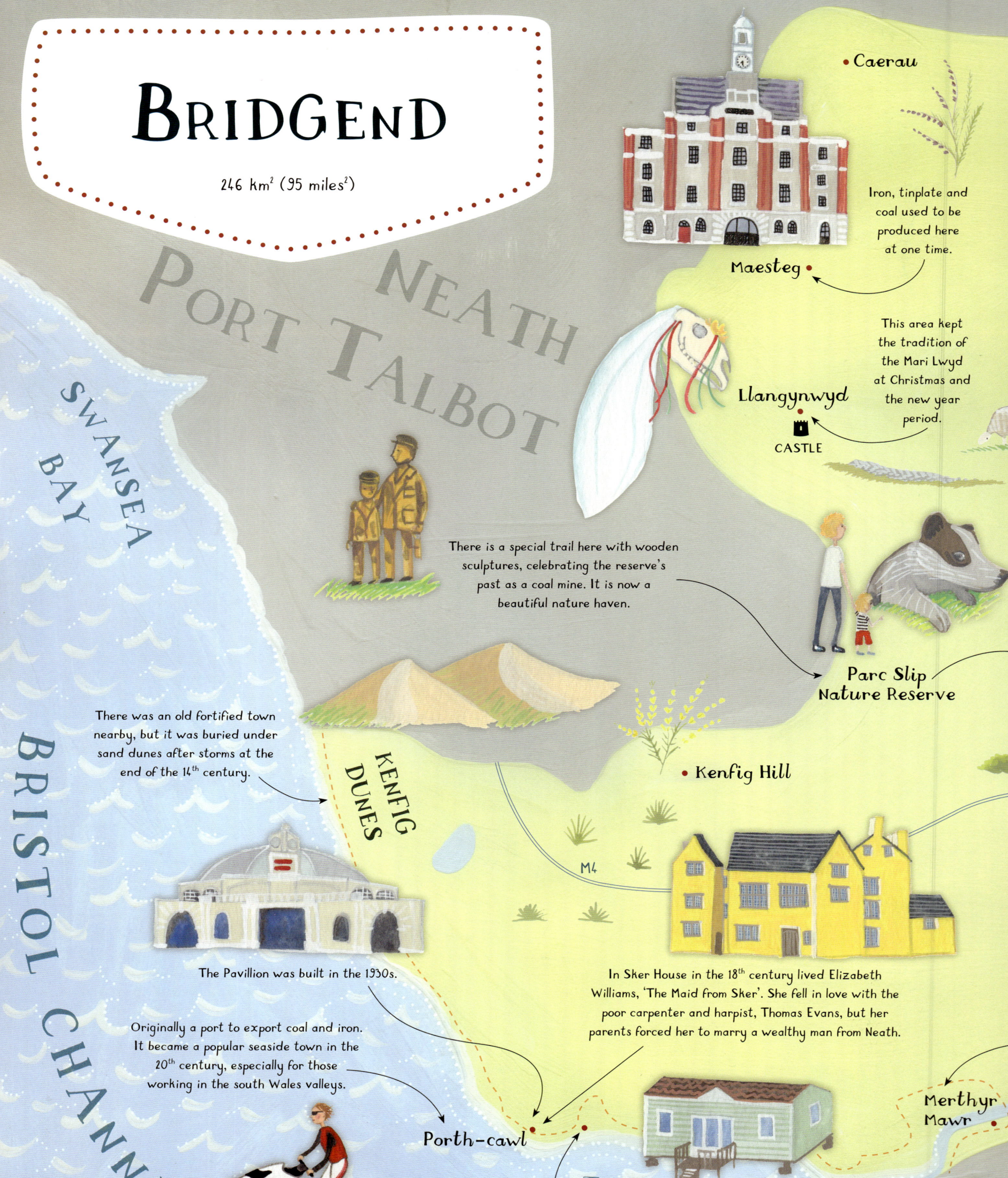

BRIDGEND

246 km² (95 miles²)

Caerau

Iron, tinplate and coal used to be produced here at one time.

Maesteg

This area kept the tradition of the Mari Lwyd at Christmas and the new year period.

Llangynwyd

CASTLE

NEATH PORT TALBOT

SWANSEA BAY

BRISTOL CHANNEL

There is a special trail here with wooden sculptures, celebrating the reserve's past as a coal mine. It is now a beautiful nature haven.

Parc Slip Nature Reserve

There was an old fortified town nearby, but it was buried under sand dunes after storms at the end of the 14th century.

KENFIG DUNES

Kenfig Hill

M4

The Pavillion was built in the 1930s.

In Sker House in the 18th century lived Elizabeth Williams, 'The Maid from Sker'. She fell in love with the poor carpenter and harpist, Thomas Evans, but her parents forced her to marry a wealthy man from Neath.

Originally a port to export coal and iron. It became a popular seaside town in the 20th century, especially for those working in the south Wales valleys.

Porth-cawl

Merthyr Mawr

TRECCO BAY

The caravan park in Trecco Bay is one of the largest in Europe.

BRIDGEND
POPULATION ABOUT
145,500
★ ★ ★

Nant-y-moel

Pontycymer

Lynn Davies from Nant-y-moel won an Olympic long jump gold medal in Tokyo in 1964. He was the first Welshman to win an individual athletics Olympic gold medal.

There are many factories and businesses in the area as it is close to the M4 motorway.

Llangeinor

McArthurGlen is a large centre with shops, a cinema and restaurants near the M4.

Glynogwr

During the Glyndŵr Uprising, the castle was under siege twice between 1404 and 1405.

RIVER OGMORE

M4

Sarn

CASTLE
Coity

NEWCASTLE CASTLE
Bridgend

Island Farm
Camp

Newcastle Castle was built by Henry II in the 1180s.

Aled Siôn Davies is a Paralympian athlete who has been World Champion in throwing events and has won many gold medals in Paralympic Games.

Prisoners from Germany were held here during the Second World War. They built a tunnel and in March 1945, more prisoners managed to escape from here than any other prison. They were all caught.

A pretty village which has many thatched cottages and houses. There are sand dunes nearby.

33

VALE OF GLAMORGAN

335 km² (129 miles²)

BRIDGEND

RIVER OGMORE

Ewenny has been famous for making pottery for centuries. There are still two potteries here.

Ewenny

An important borough since the Middle Ages. A part of the old town walls can still be seen. It's a popular town for shopping today.

M4

■ CASTLE
Ogmore-by-sea

Ewenny Priory was founded in the 12th century. A painting by the famous artist, J. M. W. Turner, shows the priory at the end of the 18th century.

Cowbridge

LLANBLETHIAN ■
CASTLE

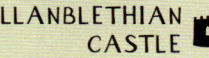 Llandow

On Bryn Owain, Iolo Morganwg held the first Gorsedd in Wales in 1795.

Fossils are seen on the beach here.

Wick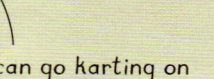

You can go karting on Llandow Racing Circuit.

WALES COAST PATH

Illtud, the saint, had an important cloister here from the end of the 5th century.

Aston Martin has a car-making factory here.

Llantwit Major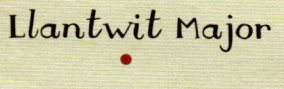

St Athan ✈

In the summer, you can go on trips on pleasure steamers from Penarth pier.

BRISTOL CHANNEL

34

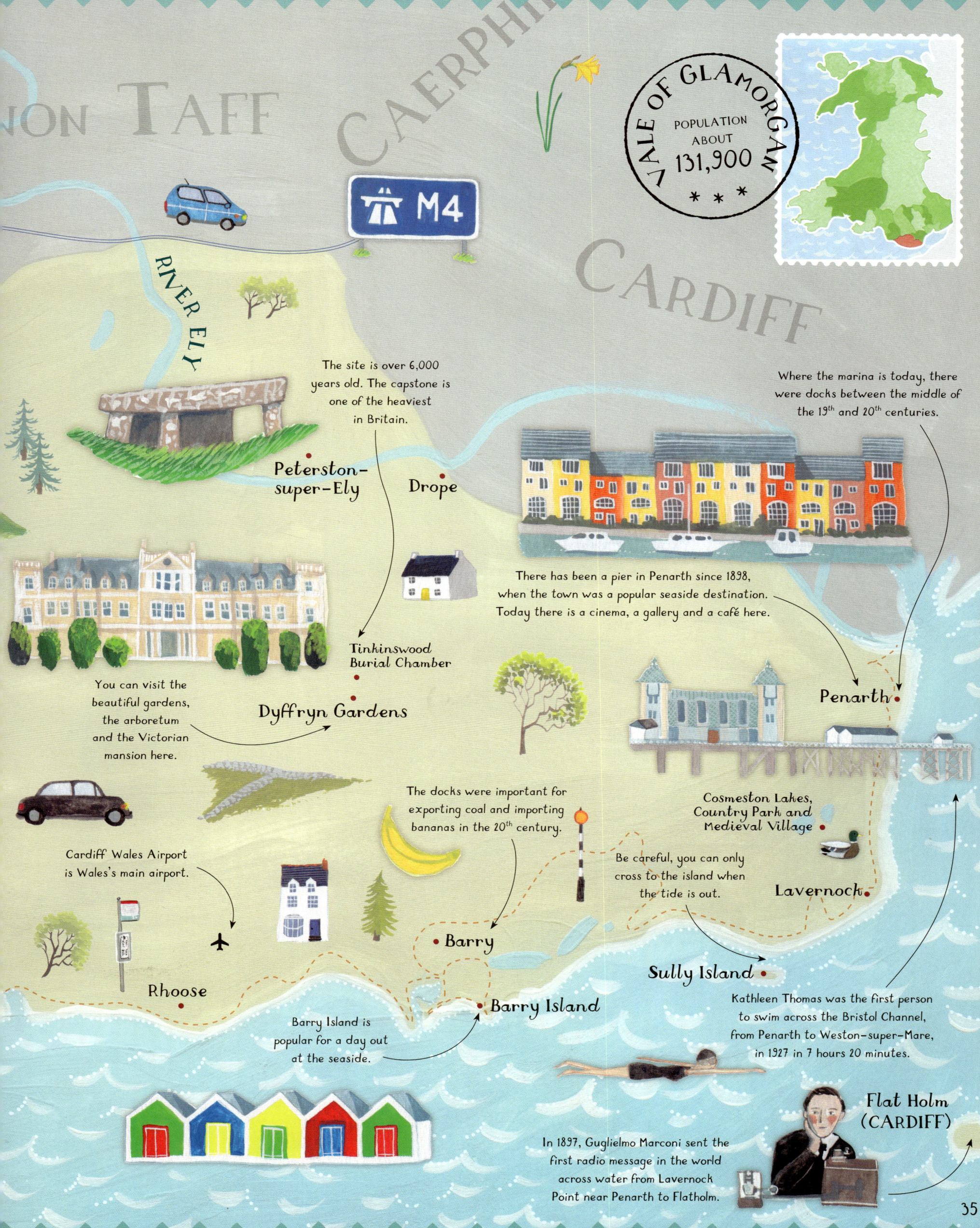

NON **TAFF** CAERPHII CARDIFF

M4

RIVER ELY

The site is over 6,000 years old. The capstone is one of the heaviest in Britain.

Peterston-super-Ely

Drope

Where the marina is today, there were docks between the middle of the 19th and 20th centuries.

There has been a pier in Penarth since 1898, when the town was a popular seaside destination. Today there is a cinema, a gallery and a café here.

Tinkinswood Burial Chamber

You can visit the beautiful gardens, the arboretum and the Victorian mansion here.

Dyffryn Gardens

Penarth

Cosmeston Lakes, Country Park and Medieval Village

The docks were important for exporting coal and importing bananas in the 20th century.

Be careful, you can only cross to the island when the tide is out.

Lavernock

Cardiff Wales Airport is Wales's main airport.

Barry

Rhoose

Barry Island is popular for a day out at the seaside.

Barry Island

Sully Island

Kathleen Thomas was the first person to swim across the Bristol Channel, from Penarth to Weston-super-Mare, in 1927 in 7 hours 20 minutes.

Flat Holm
(CARDIFF)

In 1897, Guglielmo Marconi sent the first radio message in the world across water from Lavernock Point near Penarth to Flatholm.

35

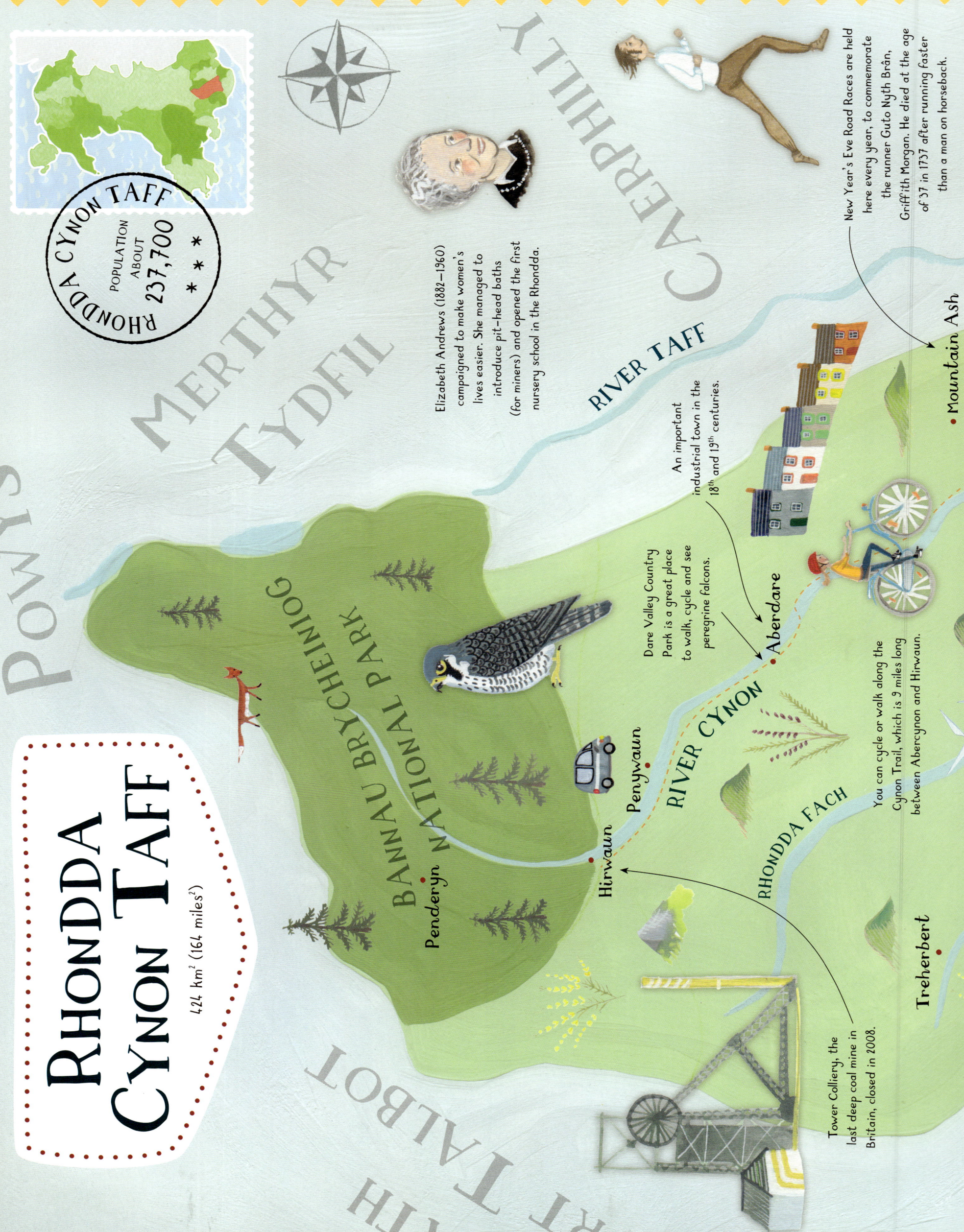

RHONDDA CYNON TAFF

424 km² (164 miles²)

POWYS

MERTHYR TYDFIL

CAERPHILLY

NEATH PORT TALBOT

Elizabeth Andrews (1882–1960) campaigned to make women's lives easier. She managed to introduce pit-head baths (for miners) and opened the first nursery school in the Rhondda.

New Year's Eve Road Races are held here every year, to commemorate the runner Guto Nyth Brân, Griffith Morgan. He died at the age of 37 in 1737 after running faster than a man on horseback.

RIVER TAFF

• Mountain Ash

An important industrial town in the 18th and 19th centuries.

Dare Valley Country Park is a great place to walk, cycle and see peregrine falcons.

• Aberdare

RIVER CYNON

You can cycle or walk along the Cynon Trail, which is 9 miles long between Abercynon and Hirwaun.

BANNAU BRYCHEINIOG NATIONAL PARK

Penderyn •

• Penywaun

RHONDDA FACH

Hirwaun •

• Treherbert

Tower Colliery, the last deep coal mine in Britain, closed in 2008.

There is a memorial in Ynysangharad Park to Evan and James James. The father and son composed the national anthem, 'Hen Wlad fy Nhadau', in 1856.

Ysgol Gyfun Rhydfelen, the first Welsh-medium comprehensive in south Wales, opened near Pontypridd in 1962. It changed its name to Ysgol Garth Olwg when it moved to Church Village in 2006.

• **Nantgarw**

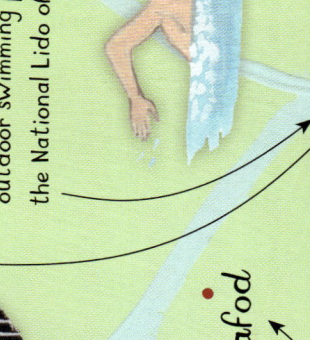

Abercynon

Sir Tom Jones, the world-famous singer, comes from Pontypridd.

Ponty Lido, with its three outdoor swimming pools, is the National Lido of Wales.

• **Pontypridd**

The town is famous for the old bridge built by William Edwards in 1756. It has a single span of 42.3m.

Llantwit Fardre

In Nantgarw Chinaworks Museum, you can see the wonderful porcelain produced here between 1813 and 1820.

Trehafod •

RIVER RHONDDA

Porth •

• **Ferndale**

178 miners were killed in an explosion here in 1867, and a further 53 were killed in 1869.

■ CASTLE

Llantrisant •

Pontyclun •

RIVER ELY

Tonyrefail •

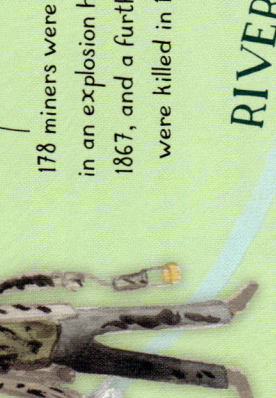

Treorchy •

Tonypandy •

During the riots here in 1910, miners who were striking for more pay damaged over 60 shops in the main street.

Many people moved to the area to work in the ironworks and coalmines in the 19th and 20th centuries.

How about going underground at the old Lewis Merthyr Colliery in Rhondda Heritage Park?

Llanharan •

You can visit the Royal Mint which produces all the coins for the UK and many other countries.

M4

VALE OF GLAMORGAN

BRIDGEND

Merthyr Tydfil is the county which has the smallest population in Wales. But in 1851, when Merthyr was the capital of iron production, it was the town with the largest population in Wales.

In the 1840s, Dowlais Iron Company's ironworks was the largest in the world, with 5,000 workers.

Lady Charlotte Guest (1812–95) was the wife of the owner of Dowlais Ironworks. She translated the tales of the Mabinogi from Welsh into English.

The chains for the Menai Bridge (Anglesey) were made in Penydarren ironworks.

Julien Macdonald, the fashion designer, comes originally from Merthyr.

MERTHYR TYDFIL
POPULATION ABOUT **58,800**

Morlais Castle was built in the 1280s by Gilbert de Clare.

There was a Roman fort here around AD 75.

POWYS

PONTSTICILL RESERVOIR

Pontsticill

MORLAIS CASTLE

Pant

Dowlais

Penydarren

Merthyr Tydfil

BANNAU BRYCHEINIOG NATIONAL PARK

TAF FECHAN

BRECON MOUNTAIN RAILWAY

Brecon Mountain Railway's main station is here.

Cefncoedycymer

Park

You can visit the cottage where Joseph Parry (1841–1903) was born. He composed the song 'Myfanwy'.

There is a low ropes course here.

Garwnant Visitor Centre

LLWYN-ONN RESERVOIR

Cyfarthfa Castle is a Museum and Art Gallery today. But the huge mansion house was originally home to the Crawshay family, the Merthyr ironmasters.

TAF FAWR

In 1804, Richard Trevithich experimented for the first time in the world with a steam locomotive. The engine travelled at 8km per hour, over 14km from Merthyr to Navigation on the Glamorganshire Canal. It pulled 10 metric tonnes of iron and around 70 passengers.

• Bedlinog

A terrible disaster happened here on 21 October 1966. Coal waste from Merthyr Vale colliery slid down and destroyed a farm, houses, Pant-glas primary school and a part of the secondary school. 116 children and 28 adults were killed.

• Trelewis

• Treharris

There is a climbing centre in the old Trelewis colliery, with 18-metre high walls.

Keir Hardie became Britain's first socialist member of parliament in 1900. He originally came from Scotland

RIVER TAFF

Hoover had a large factory in Merthyr between 1948 and 2009.

Aberfan •

There is a mountain biking centre in the area.

MERTHYR TYDFIL

111 km² (43 miles²)

Merthyr is famous for producing textiles.

Laura Ashley, the fashion designer, was born in Merthyr.

Tydfil, daughter of King Brychan from the 5th century, was a saint.

There is a statue in the town to remember the boxer Johnny Owen, the bantamweight boxing champion of Wales, Britain, the Commonwealth and Europe. He died after falling into a coma during a world-championship fight in Los Angeles in 1980.

Another famous boxer from the county is World Champion Featherweight Howard Winstone, and the trainer for both boxers was Eddie Thomas.

The Taff Trail is a popular cycle path, 55 miles long, from Cardiff Bay to Brecon.

Castell Coch, as we know it today, was built at the end of the 19th century to a design by William Burges, but there has been a castle here since the 12th century.

CASTELL COCH

Tongwynlais

Pentyrch

Capital of Wales since 1955. A third of the population of Wales lives in the Cardiff city area.

Radyr

RIVER TAFF

Sophia Gardens is the home of Glamorgan County Cricket Club.

M4

In the cathedral, there is a huge concrete arch supporting *Majestas*, Jacob Epstein's statue.

A Tudor castle was built here in the 1580s. The Museum of Welsh Life has been here since 1947.

Llandaff

VALE OF GLAMORGAN

St Fagans

RIVER ELY

Sophia Gardens

Arms Park

Cardiff International Sports Stadium

Home of Cardiff City football club.

Cardiff City Stadium

Gareth Bale, the world famous footballer, comes from Cardiff.

Arms Park is home of Cardiff Rugby regional rugby team. The Welsh rugby team used to play here before the Principality Stadium was built.

The stadium which opened in 1999 seats 74,500 people. Its original name was the Millennium Stadium.

CITY AND COUNTY OF
CARDIFF

140 km² (54 miles²)

Shree Swaminarayan Mandir is the first and largest Hindu temple to be built in Wales.

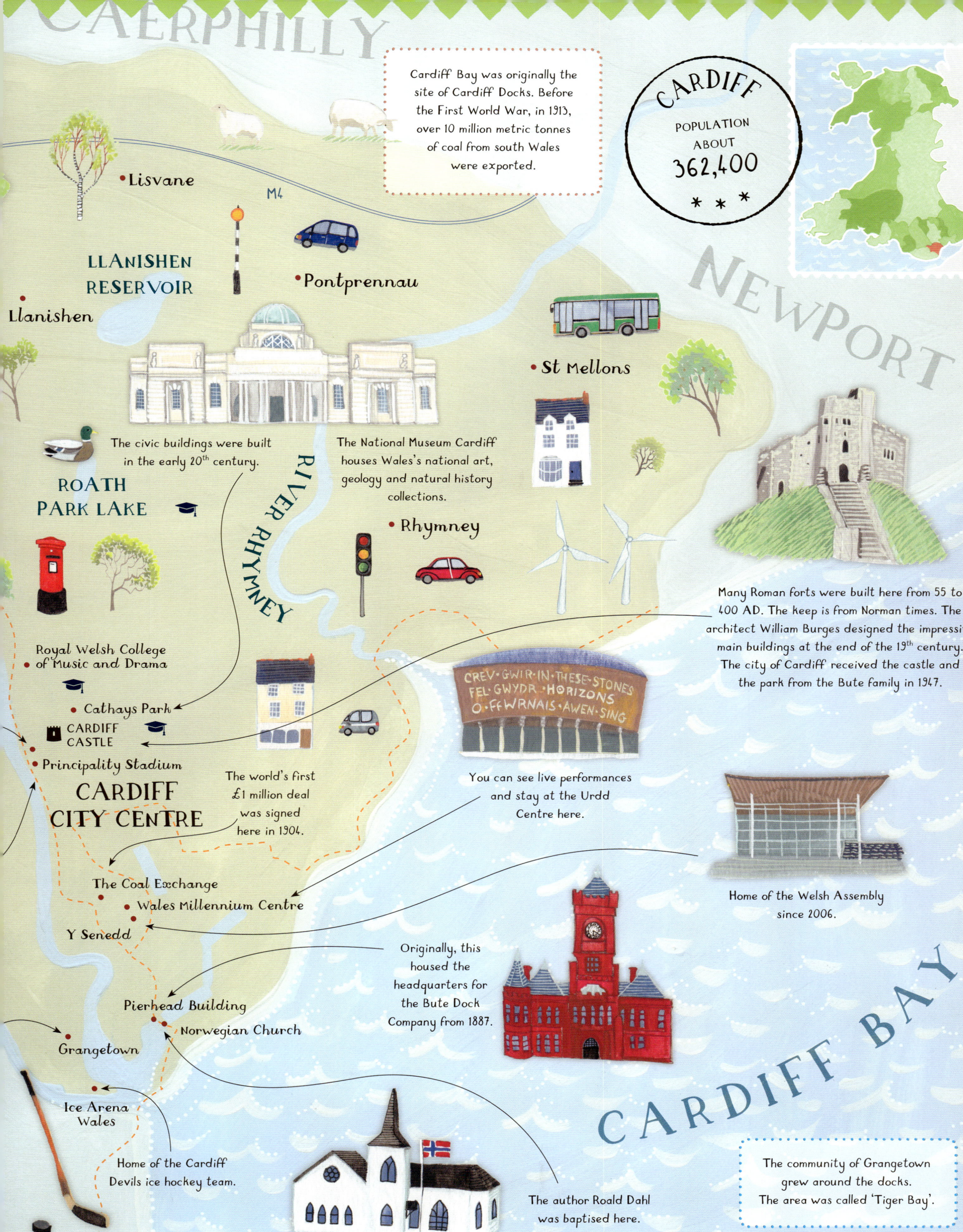

CAERPHILLY

41

NEWPORT

CARDIFF BAY

Cardiff Bay was originally the site of Cardiff Docks. Before the First World War, in 1913, over 10 million metric tonnes of coal from south Wales were exported.

CARDIFF
POPULATION ABOUT
362,400
★ ★ ★

• Lisvane

M4

LLANISHEN RESERVOIR

• Pontprennau

Llanishen

ROATH PARK LAKE

The civic buildings were built in the early 20th century.

The National Museum Cardiff houses Wales's national art, geology and natural history collections.

• St Mellons

• Rhymney

RIVER RHYMNEY

Royal Welsh College of Music and Drama

• Cathays Park

CARDIFF CASTLE

• Principality Stadium

CARDIFF CITY CENTRE

The world's first £1 million deal was signed here in 1904.

Many Roman forts were built here from 55 to 400 AD. The keep is from Norman times. The architect William Burges designed the impressive main buildings at the end of the 19th century. The city of Cardiff received the castle and the park from the Bute family in 1947.

CREV·GWIR·IN·THESE·STONES
FEL·GWYDR·HORIZONS
O·FFWRNAIS·AWEN·SING

You can see live performances and stay at the Urdd Centre here.

Home of the Welsh Assembly since 2006.

The Coal Exchange

• Wales Millennium Centre

Y Senedd

Originally, this housed the headquarters for the Bute Dock Company from 1887.

Pierhead Building

• Norwegian Church

Grangetown

Ice Arena Wales

Home of the Cardiff Devils ice hockey team.

The author Roald Dahl was baptised here.

The community of Grangetown grew around the docks. The area was called 'Tiger Bay'.

CAERPHILLY

278 km² (107 miles²)

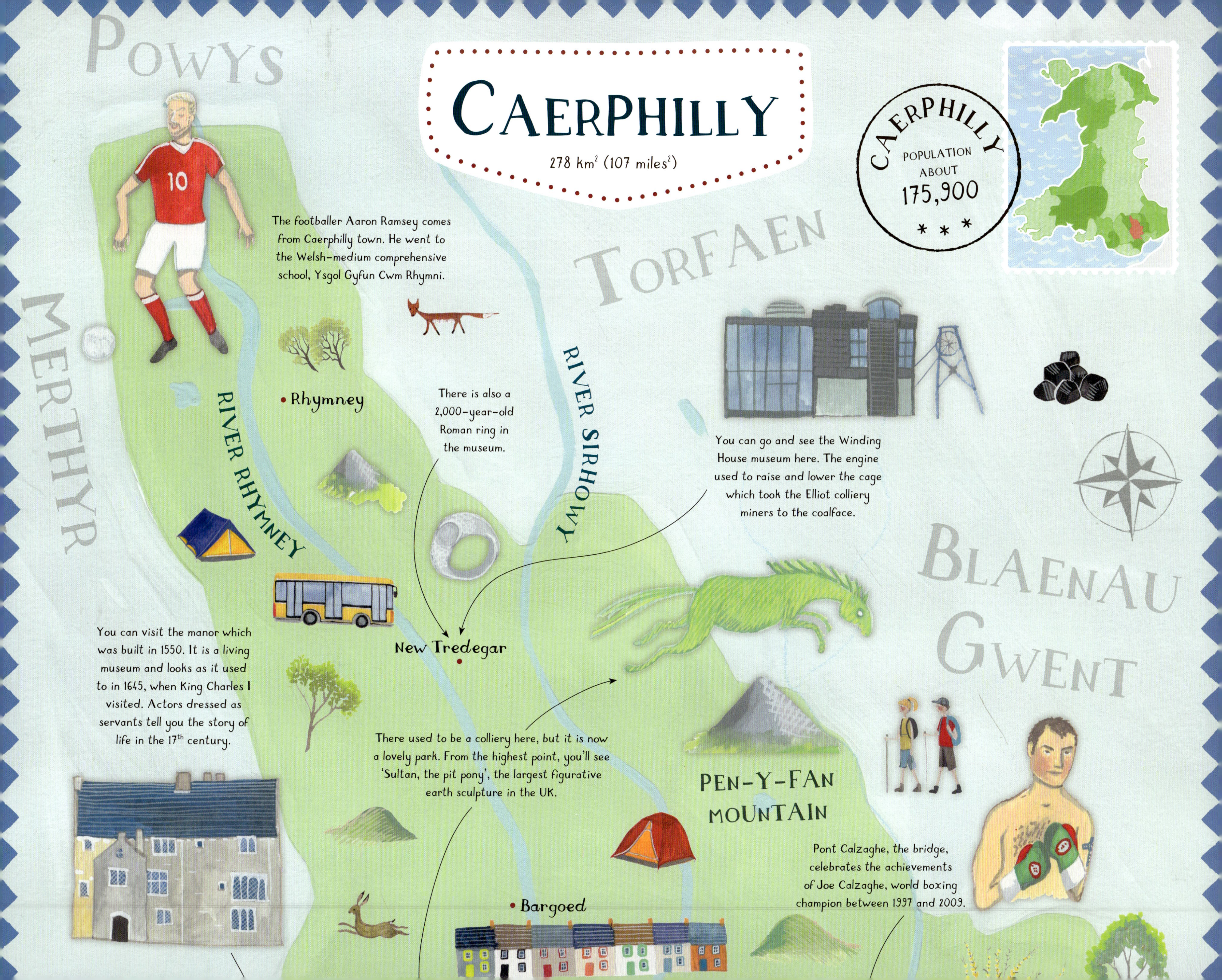

CAERPHILLY
POPULATION
ABOUT
175,900
POWYS
MERTHYR
TORFAEN
BLAENAU GWENT
RIVER RHYMNEY
RIVER SIRHOWY
Rhymney
New Tredegar
Bargoed
PEN-Y-FAN MOUNTAIN
10
The footballer Aaron Ramsey comes from Caerphilly town. He went to the Welsh-medium comprehensive school, Ysgol Gyfun Cwm Rhymni.
There is also a 2,000-year-old Roman ring in the museum.
You can go and see the Winding House museum here. The engine used to raise and lower the cage which took the Elliot colliery miners to the coalface.
You can visit the manor which was built in 1550. It is a living museum and looks as it used to in 1645, when King Charles I visited. Actors dressed as servants tell you the story of life in the 17th century.
There used to be a colliery here, but it is now a lovely park. From the highest point, you'll see 'Sultan, the pit pony', the largest figurative earth sculpture in the UK.
Pont Calzaghe, the bridge, celebrates the achievements of Joe Calzaghe, world boxing champion between 1997 and 2009.

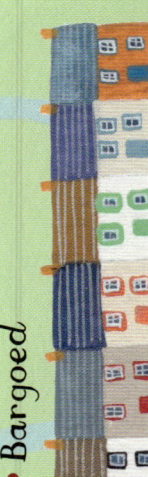

MONMOUTHSHIRE AND BRECON CANAL

RIVER EBBW

• Newbridge

• Cwm-carn

• Risca

• Machen

• Blackwood

• Penallta

Ynysddu

• Senghennydd

Caerphilly

CASTLE

CAERPHILLY MOUNTAIN

Llancaiach Fawr •

The Manic Street Preachers rock band come from here.

Lead and copper used to be mined in this area.

There is a LEGO model of Caerphilly castle at Legoland Windsor.

The south-west tower leans more than the leaning tower of Pisa!

There has been a Roman fortress here since around AD 75.

On 14 October 1913, 439 men and boys were killed in an explosion in the Universal colliery. This was the worst disaster in the history of the south Wales coalfield. The Aber Valley Heritage Museum tells the story.

The Big Cheese Festival is held at the end of July, and 80,000 people come to enjoy all kinds of entertainment.

Coalminers used to like white Caerphilly cheese. There is a model of a Caerphilly cheese on a roundabout in the town.

Caerphilly castle is the largest in Wales and the second largest in Britain after Windsor castle. It extends over 12 hectares. Gilbert de Clare began the building work in 1268. The work was stopped for a while in 1270 when Llywelyn ap Gruffudd attacked. In 1316, Llywelyn Bren tried to capture the castle by putting it under siege with 10,000 of his men.

People say that the manor is haunted, and night-time ghost hunts are held there.

There is a statue of the comedian Tommy Cooper (1921–1984) opposite the castle. He was born in Caerphilly.

The castle has been used as a location for many television programmes and films, including Dr Who.

POLICE BOX

RHONDDA CYNON TAFF

CARDIFF

43

Beautiful furniture was made here between 1929 and 1940.

MONMOUTH

Rassau

BANNAU BRYCHEINIOG NATIONAL PARK

Bryn-mawr

Nant-y-glo

You can do all kinds of outdoor activities in Parc Bryn Bach, including canoeing, archery and climbing.

SIRHOWY RIVER

Ebbw Vale

In 1816, Joseph Bailey, the local ironmaster, built two round towers. He was afraid his workers would rebel against him. If they had done, he and his family would have gone to live in the two 'castles'.

Tredegar

The Clock Tower (1858) was made from cast iron from the local ironworks.

After the works closed, the Garden Festival of Wales was held here in 1992. Now, shops and other amenities are to be found in the Festival Park. There is an owl sanctuary is in the park and you can go down the hill on the longest tube ride in Britain!

The Ebbw Vale Steel, Iron and Coal Company's works used to extend for 5km along the valley. 34,000 men worked there at the beginning of the 20th century.

EBBW FACH

Cwm

The Ebbw Fach trail connects two lakes in Cwmtillery.

Abertillery

Aneurin Bevan (1897–1960), who established the National Health Service, was born in Tredegar.

World Champion snooker players Ray Reardon and Mark Williams come from this area.

RIVER EBBW

Six Bells

Aberbeeg

TORFAEN

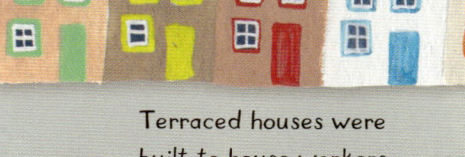

Terraced houses were built to house workers and their families.

45 men were killed in an accident at Six Bells colliery in 1960. Since 2010, there has been a memorial to commemorate this. It is called 'Guardian'.

BLAENAU GWENT

109 km² (42 miles²)

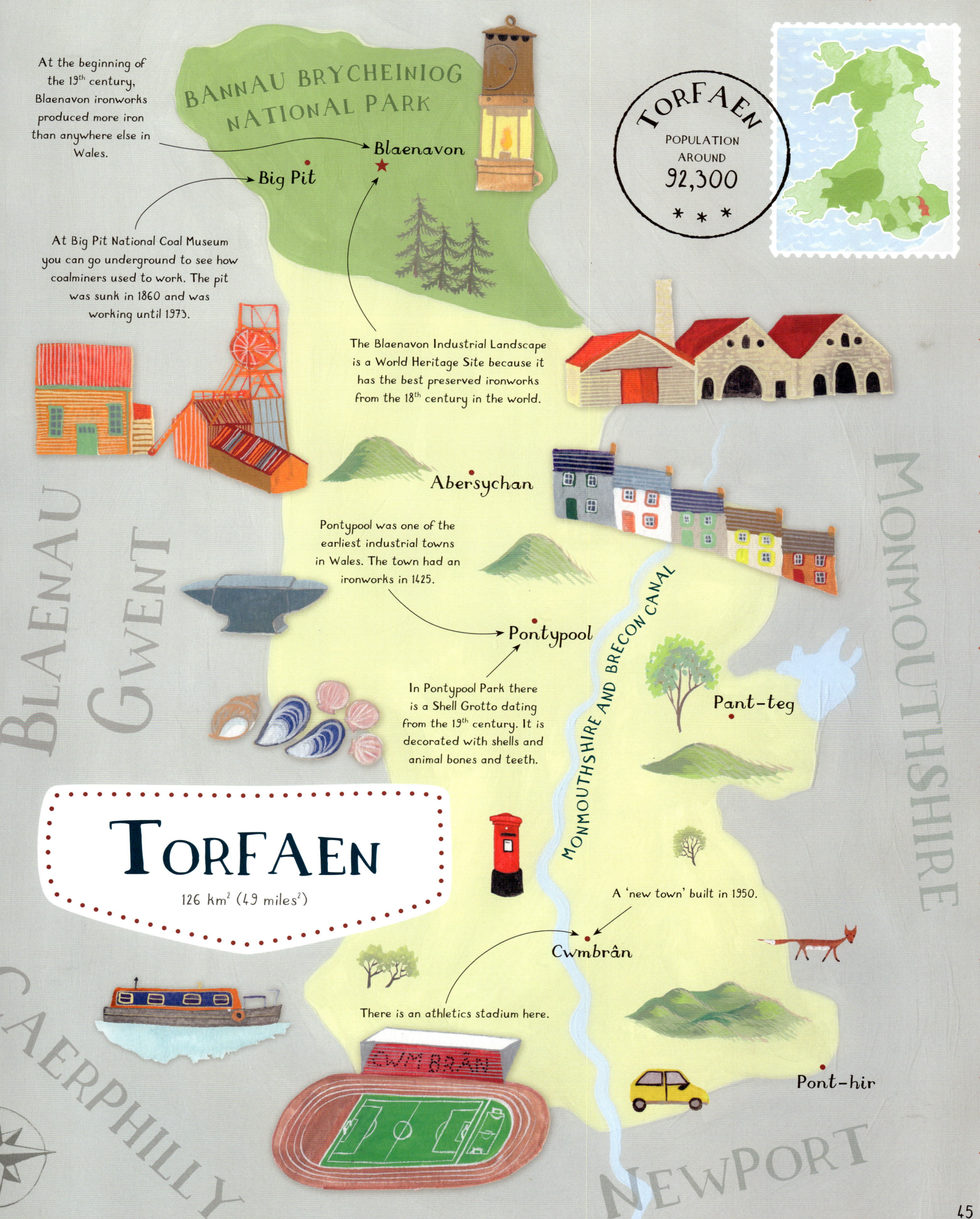

BANNAU BRYCHEINIOG NATIONAL PARK

At the beginning of the 19th century, Blaenavon ironworks produced more iron than anywhere else in Wales.

Big Pit

Blaenavon

At Big Pit National Coal Museum you can go underground to see how coalminers used to work. The pit was sunk in 1860 and was working until 1973.

The Blaenavon Industrial Landscape is a World Heritage Site because it has the best preserved ironworks from the 18th century in the world.

Abersychan

Pontypool was one of the earliest industrial towns in Wales. The town had an ironworks in 1425.

Pontypool

In Pontypool Park there is a Shell Grotto dating from the 19th century. It is decorated with shells and animal bones and teeth.

Pant-teg

MONMOUTHSHIRE AND BRECON CANAL

A 'new town' built in 1950.

Cwmbrân

There is an athletics stadium here.

Pont-hir

TORFAEN

126 km² (49 miles²)

TORFAEN

POPULATION AROUND

92,300

★ ★ ★

BLAENAU

GWENT

CAERPHILLY

MONMOUTHSHIRE

NEWPORT

45

NEWPORT

190 km² (73 miles²)

At the Caerleon Roman Fortress and Baths you get a picture of how Roman soldiers used to spend their spare time in the 2nd century.

Owain Glyndŵr attacked Newport castle in 1402.

The Romans established a fort in AD 75 and there were soldiers stationed here for over 200 years. The National Roman Legion Museum shows how they used to live, fight, worship and die.

Newport has been a city since 2002.

In Westgate Square, there is a sculpture to commemorate the Chartists' Rising in 1839. 5,000 armed Chartists marched to the Westgate Hotel. They were protesting for the right for all men to have the vote. They were defeated after a 25-minute battle with soldiers. John Frost, the leader, was transported to Van Diemen's Land, now called Tasmania.

CAERPHILLY

CARDIFF

RIVER EBBW

MONMOUTHSHIRE AND BRECON CANAL

Bettws

The Old Green Mural, made from mosaic and concrete, depicts how important the railway and canal were for Newport in the 19th century.

Rogerstone

RIVER USK

CASTLE

Rodney Parade

NEWPORT CITY CENTRE

Bassaleg

The saint Gwynllyw established a church on Stow Hill in the 6th century. St Woolos Cathedral stands here today.

Tredegar House

An important merchant ship from the middle of the 15th century was found in 2002 in mud on the banks of the river Usk.

ALEXANDRA DOCKS

M4

A48(M)

How about visiting Tredegar House, the home of the Morgan family from 1660 to 1951? The gardens and the park are also worth a visit.

46

ORFAEN

World leaders stayed at the Celtic Manor Resort when the NATO summit was held there in 2014.

The Ryder Cup, an important golf competition, was held in Newport in 2010.

Llanvaches

Penhow

NEWPORT POPULATION ABOUT 159,600 ★ ★ ★

Caerleon

M4   Celtic Manor

MONMOUTHSHIRE

Rodney Parade is the home of the Dragons regional rugby club and Newport County football club.

In the 19th century, some people claimed that Newport was in England.

Liswerry

RUGBY

The Steel Wave sculpture by Peter Fink is on the banks of the river Usk.

Wales National Velodrome

Many famous cyclists have trained at the Wales National Velodrome.

You can climb up and across the Transporter Bridge, or be transported across in a gondola. It was built in 1906.

WALES COAST PATH

ash

Whitson

Newport Wetlands RSPB nature reserve is a great place to watch birds and wildlife and see the old East Usk lighthouse.

In the 1830s, Newport was the main port for exporting coal from south Wales.

BRISTOL CHANNEL

47

ENGLA[ND]

RIVER WYE

The gate tower on the bridge is part of the old town walls. This is the only one remaining in Britain where the gate actually stands on a medieval river bridge.

CASTLE · Monmouth

Rochfield

MONMOUTHSHIRE
POPULATION ABOUT 93,000

There is a world-famous recording studio here.

Skenfrith · CASTLE

Henry V was born in the castle here in 1387.

Raglan CASTLE

RIVER MONNOW

CASTLE · Grosmont

The castle was built between the 15th and early 17th century. Henry Tudor (Henry VII) spent his childhood here.

There is a statue of Charles Rolls (1877–1910) in Agincourt Square, Monmouth. His family home was near the town. He established the Rolls-Royce car company with Henry Royce in 1904. In June 1910, he was the first to fly across the Channel to France and back without landing. Also, a month later, he was the first to be killed in an aeroplane accident in Britain.

Llanthony

Tens of thousands of people come to the food festival here every September.

CASTLE · Abergavenny

MONMOUTHSHIRE AND BRECON CANAL

You can do all kinds of activities in the Outdoor Education Centre here. How about canoeing on the Monmouthshire and Brecon Canal?

Gilwern

POWYS

TOR[FAEN]

RIVER WYE

Tintern Abbey

An abbey was built here in 1131. It was one of the richest in Wales.

There is a racecourse here.

Chepstow ■ CASTLE

Severn Bridge

SEVERN TUNNEL

Prince of Wales Bridge

76,400,100 bricks were used to build the railway tunnel. It's nearly 7km long. The first train travelled through in 1885 and the first passengers in 1886. For 100 years, this was the longest underwater railway tunnel in the world.

ENGLAND

In 1568, brass was produced for the first time in Britain in a foundry in Tintern.

■ CASTLE

Ush

The castle (1067) is important because it's the oldest building in Wales which doesn't belong to the church. In 2013, a special *Dr Who* programme was filmed here to celebrate the series' 50th anniversary.

Caerwent

A48(M)

■ CALDICOT CASTLE

M4

M4

RIVER USK

Owain Glyndŵr's forces were defeated at the Battle of Pwll Melyn in 1405.

The famous naturalist Alfred Russel Wallace (1823–1913) was born here.

The first bridge was opened in 1966. Before then, cars crossed the river Severn on a ferry. The bridge won many awards for its design. Its two towers are 125m in height.

The second bridge, the Prince of Wales Bridge, was opened in 1996. It spans 5km across the river.

BRISTOL CHANNEL

You can see 5-metre-high town walls from Roman times (around AD 180) here.

NEWPORT

From 2018, drivers don't have to pay a toll to cross the Severn Bridge.

AEN

MONMOUTHSHIRE
850 km² (330 miles²)

FOLKLORE AND TRADITIONS

ENGLAND

St Asaph
Dic Aberdaron wandered around Wales and England, barefoot and long haired, carrying a harp, books and a cat. He could speak 14 languages! He died in 1843 and is buried in St Asaph.

NORTH-EAST WALES

Dancing, carrying the maypole and Cadi Haf collecting money on May Day.

• **Bala**
Llyn Tegid (Bala Lake)

Pennant Melangell
Saint Melangell and Prince Brochwel

Rhita the Ogre
Shaved the beards of other kings and wove them onto his cloak.

• Gelert
Dinas Emrys
The battle between the red dragon and the white dragon

Yr Wyddfa (Snowdon)

Beddgelert

• **Caernarfon**

Nantlle Valley
Blodeuwedd

ANGLESEY

Cadair Idris
If you spend the night here, you will either be a poet or mad when you wake up.

• **Devil's Bridge**

Ceridwen the sorceress
Taliesin

Porthmadog
Madog ab Owain Gwynedd who went to America around 1170

LLŶN PENINSULA

Nant Gwrtheyrn
Rhys and Meinir

• **Aber-soch**
March ap Meirchion's Ears

Macsen's Dream

• Aberdaron

CARDIGAN BAY

Tristan and Isolde

Seiriol Wyn and Cybi Felyn

Bardsey Island •
King Arthur and Merlin the wizard are said to be buried here.

IRISH SEA

Plygain
People gather to sing and listen to carols during the Christmas and New Year period.

Ghost, or 'Bwci Bo' in Welsh.

Excalibur, King Arthur's sword, was thrown into Llyn Llydaw on Yr Wyddfa (Snowdon).

POWYS

Mountain Ash
Guto Nyth Brân

The 'Mari Lwyd'

Myddfai
The Physicians of Myddfai

• Llyn y Fan Fach
The Lady of the Lake

Tregaron •

Llanddewibrefi
St David and the hill which rose beneath him so people could see him.

Ystrad-ffin •
Twm Siôn Cati

• Amman Valley
Trwyth the Boar

• Ynysforgan

Llangynwyd

The Old Man of Pencader

The Red Book of Hergest

• Pencader

The Wyvern of Newcastle Emlyn
The Wyvern fell into the river after it was struck by an arrow; the river was poisoned by its body and all the fish were killed.

Carmarthen •
Merlin the wizard's Old Oak

Gorslas •
Llyn Llech Owain

Newcastle Emlyn •

• Kidwelly

'Hen Fenyw Fach Cydweli' who used to sell black sweets.

Cantre'r Gwaelod

Bendigeidfran

Branwen's starling

Gwaun Valley •
Calennig: Children go to people's houses wishing them a Happy New Year.

Pwyll, Prince of Dyfed

'Black Bart', a pirate from Little Newcastle

Narberth •

Grassholm
An island off the coast of Pembrokeshire. A feast with the head of Bendigeidfran the giant.

BRISTOL CHANNEL

51

THE ARTS

Hedd Wyn was killed before he knew that he had won the chair in the National Eisteddfod. He is known as the 'Bard of the Black Chair'.

Poets

Gillian Clarke

There was a poet in every court during the time of the Welsh kings and princes. Poets were paid to write poems.

A new Bardd Plant Cymru (Welsh Children's Poet) is chosen every two years.

People all over the world enjoy the poetry of Dylan Thomas (1914–53), R. S. Thomas (1913–2000), Gillian Clarke and Owen Sheers in English.

Hanan Issa became the National Poet of Wales in 2022.

R. S. Thomas

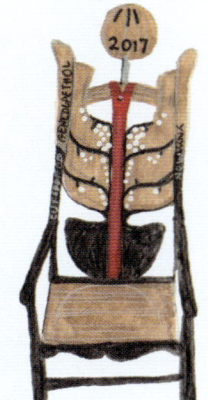

Cynghanedd poetry in Welsh is unique. It has rhyme and alliteration patterns. The chair in the National Eisteddfod is the prize for the best cynghanedd poem.

The National Eisteddfod is a huge cultural festival and it takes place every year during the first week of August.

Mererid Hopwood

Mererid Hopwood is the first woman to win the chair at the National Eisteddfod.

The Urdd Eisteddfod is Europe's largest youth festival.

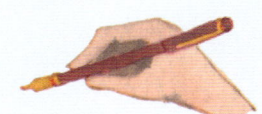

Artists

Famous Welsh artists include Sir Kyffin Williams (1918–2006) from Anglesey, Aneurin Jones (1930–2017) from Cardigan and Josef Herman (1911–2000), who came to live in Ystradgynlais from Poland, in 1944. Charles Tunnicliffe (1901–79), who lived on Anglesey, and brother and sister Augustus John (1878–1961) and Gwen John (1876–1939) from Pembrokeshire.

Famous artists such as J. M. W. Turner (1775–1851) came to Wales to paint landscapes.

Charles Tunnicliffe

Authors

T. Llew Jones

The Welsh author Kate Roberts (1891–1985) from Rhosgadfan, Caernarfon, is known as 'The queen of our literature'.

Popular children's authors from Wales include T. Llew Jones (1915–2009) in Welsh and Roald Dahl (1916–1990) in English.

Kate Roberts

Roald Dahl

Sir Kyffin Williams

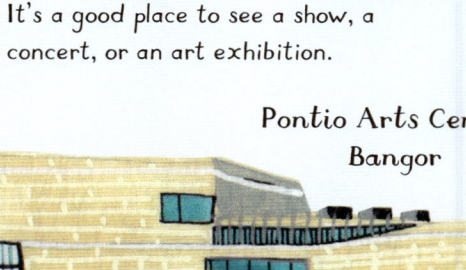

Aberystwyth Arts Centre

Where is your local **arts centre**? It's a good place to see a show, a concert, or an art exhibition.

Actors

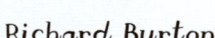

Richard Burton

Many excellent actors come from Wales. Some, such as Matthew Rhys and Ioan Gruffudd from Cardiff, and Anthony Hopkins and Richard Burton (1925–84) from the Port Talbot area, have also become stars in the USA. Catherine Zeta-Jones, who is originally from Swansea, has won an Oscar for acting. Michael Sheen, the famous actor, was brought up in Baglan.

Sir Anthony Hopkins

Pontio Arts Centre, Bangor

Male Voice Choirs

Catrin
Finch

Sir Tom Jones

The harp is the national instrument of Wales. The traditional harp is the triple harp, which has three rows of strings. Catrin Finch, originally from Ceredigion, is one of the best harpists in the world.

Singing

Wales is the 'land of song' and many people enjoy singing in choirs.

Some Welsh singers are famous worldwide.

Sir Bryn Terfel

Dame
Shirley Bassey

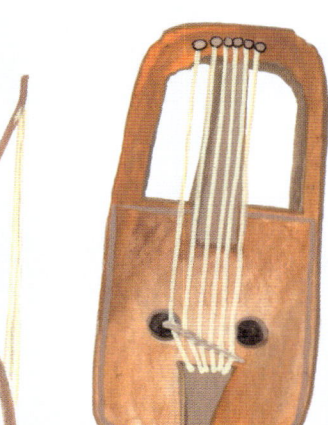

The 'crwth' was an old Welsh instrument. It was similar to a violin, played with a bow but having six strings.

Folk singing and 'cerdd dant' (singing with the harp) is very popular.

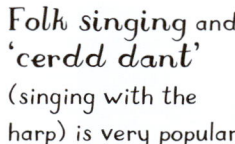

Kizzy Crawford

There are Welsh and English pop groups in Wales.

Manic Street Preachers

Composers

Sir Karl Jenkins

Sir Karl Jenkins, from Pen-clawdd near Swansea, and William Mathias (1934–92) from Whitland are well-known composers.

William Mathias

There are brass bands all over Wales, especially where there used to be coal mines, slate quarries or iron works.

All kinds of dancing are popular in Wales: disco dancing, folk dancing and clog dancing. Some people celebrate St David's Day by having a 'twmpath dawns', with Welsh folk dancing.

The Welsh Costume

Augusta Hall (1802–96) lived in Llanover Hall. She was interested in Welsh music and dancing and she developed the Welsh costume. She was married to Benjamin Hall. He organised the work of building a large clock at Westminster, London, and it was named after him – Big Ben.

SPORTS

Football is the most popular sport in Wales. The Football Association of Wales was established in 1876.

Six teams from Wales play in English leagues: Swansea, Cardiff, Newport, Wrexham, Colwyn Bay and Merthyr.

16 teams will play in the Welsh Premier League from the 2026/27 season.

Rugby was played for the first time in Wales at Llandovery and Lampeter colleges around 1850.

Neil Jenkins

The **Welsh Rugby Union** was established in 1881. By now there are rugby union and rugby league clubs all over the country.

There are four regional rugby clubs in Wales: Llanelli Scarlets, Swansea Neath Ospreys, Cardiff Blues and Gwent Dragons.

International games are played in the **Principality Stadium** in Cardiff.

Women's rugby is very popular. The Wales women's team competes in the World Cup.

Gareth Bale

The Wales **men's team** succeeded in reaching the semi-finals of Euro 2016.

The Wales **women's team** also compete at international level and made history in 2025 by qualifying for a major tournament, the UEFA Women's EURO 2025, for the first time.

Chris Coleman
Manager of the Wales football team between 2012 and 2017.

Cricket has been played in Wales since 1783. Glamorgan County Cricket Club was formed in 1888. In 1968, on St Helen's ground, Swansea, Gary Sobers from the West Indies hit six sixes in one over. He was the first ever player to do this.

An early version of **lawn tennis** was first played in Llanelidan, Denbighshire, in 1873.

Vindico Arena is the home of the Cardiff Devils **ice hockey** team.

Before the days of rugby and football, **bando** and **cnapan** were popular games.

Bando was very similar to hockey, with a stick used to hit a ball. It was played in places such as the beach behind the site of the Port Talbot steelworks today.

Cnapan was more similar to rugby. The cnapan was the name of the wooden ball, about the size of a cricket ball. Players ran with it, kicked it and threw it. Sometimes two teams of hundreds of people played a game between two villages.

Aled Siôn Davies

Bando

Cnapan

Lyn Davies

Welsh athletics champions include Colin Jackson in the 110 metre hurdles, Lyn Davies in the long jump, Dame Tanni Grey-Thompson in wheelchair racing and Aled Siôn Davies in Paralympic throwing events.

There are **judo** and **taekwon-do** clubs throughout Wales. Jade Jones from Flint has won gold medals in taekwon-do in the Olympic Games.

Jade Jones

Surfing is very popular in Wales.

Surf lifesaving is an important sport, with clubs dotted around the coast.

The **National Sailing Academy** is at Plas Heli, Pwllheli.

You can learn to **sail**, **canoe** and **windsurf** at Plas Menai, the Wales **National Outdoor Centre**.

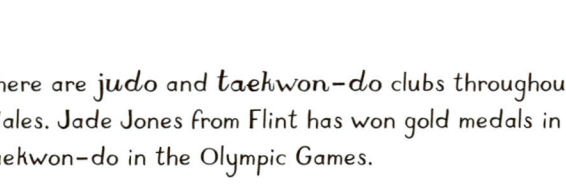

People go canoeing, sailing and white-water rafting in the Bala area.
Rowing is possible on some Welsh rivers, and on the sea.

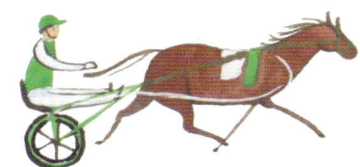

There are horse racing courses in Chepstow, Ffos Las near Trimsaran, Llanelli, and Bangor-on-Dee near Wrexham.

Wales is a great place for walking, with plenty of paths in the mountains, the valleys and along the coast. The Wales Coast Path is 870 miles long.

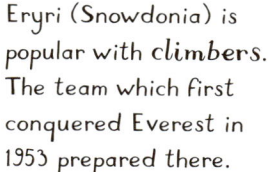

Eryri (Snowdonia) is popular with climbers. The team which first conquered Everest in 1953 prepared there.

Paulo Radmilovic, a Cardiff-born swimmer and water polo star, won four golds over three Olympics between 1908 and 1920.

Wales's caves attract cavers and pot-holers.

Nicole Cooke

There are many cycle routes in Wales. The longest two are the Celtic Trail (220 miles) from Fishguard to Chepstow, and Lôn Las Cymru (257 miles) from Cardiff to Holyhead.

The Velothon Wales race is held on one day in June or July.

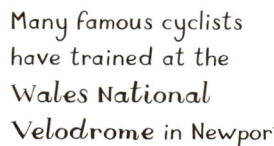

Mountain biking is popular all over Wales, with centres such as Coed-y-brenin, near Dolgellau.

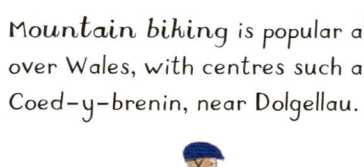

There are golf courses all over Wales. In 2010, the Ryder Cup competition came to the Newport area.

Many famous cyclists have trained at the Wales National Velodrome in Newport.

In 2018, Geraint Thomas became the first Welshman to win the Tour de France.

Many boxing champions have come from Wales, including Joe Calzaghe from Newbridge and Enzo Maccarinelli from Swansea.

Johnny Owen

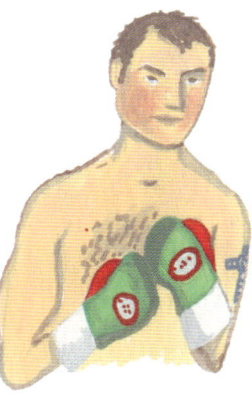

Joe Calzaghe

Rallying is very popular in Wales, with many drivers and spectators. Elfyn Evans from Dinas Mawddwy competes in the World Rally Championship.

Elfyn Evans

Many Welsh people enjoy playing or watching snooker. Mark Williams from Blaenau Gwent and Matthew Stevens from Carmarthen have been world champions.

Car and motorbike racing takes place on circuits such as those in Tŷ Croes, Anglesey, Pembrey, Carmarthenshire and Llandow, Vale of Glamorgan.

In Ruthin, there is a memorial to Tom Pryce, a 27-year-old talented racing driver who was killed in the South African Grand Prix in 1977.

Darts is popular in homes and pubs in Wales.

Tom Pryce

NATURE

You can watch osprey nests on the Cors Dyfi Reserve and on the banks of the river Glaslyn, near Porthmadog.

Osprey

The **red kite** is the national bird of Wales. It almost became extinct at the beginning of the 20th century. Now it is fairly common. You can see them being fed in some places.

RSPB Nature Reserves
The RSPB manages 18 nature reserves in Wales. They are great places to watch birds.

Many thousands of **gannets** nest on Grassholm Island in Pembrokeshire.

The short-eared owl is rare but a few pairs nest on Skomer Island.

Most of the **choughs** in Britain live in Wales. They breed on the coast of Pembrokeshire, Ceredigion, Gwynedd, Anglesey and Gower, and also in Eryri (Snowdonia).

Short-eared owl

Red Kite

Welsh dogs

Welsh sheepdogs are bigger than ordinary sheepdogs. They can be red and white, black and white or tricolour.

The Welsh **terrier** was bred to hunt animals such as mice and badgers.

There are two types of **corgis** — Pembrokeshire Corgis and Cardiganshire Corgis. Queen Elizabeth has kept Pembrokeshire Corgis since she was 18 years old.

Bardsey Apple
This was the rarest apple in the world in 2000. By now it has been cultivated and can be bought.

Snowdon Lily
The Snowdon Lily can be seen in Eryri (Snowdonia), the area of the highest mountains in Wales. This is the only place in Britain where it grows.

Snowdon Hawkweed
This is one of the rarest plants in the world. It was thought to have become extinct in the 1950s, but it was found again in Cwm Idwal, Eryri (Snowdonia), in 2002.

Tenby Daffodil

Gudgeon
This is the most famous lake fish in Wales. It lives in Llyn Tegid (Bala Lake).

Salmon
Fewer salmon live in Welsh rivers than was the case in the past.

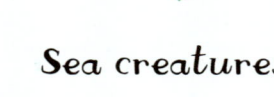

Waterlily
In June, the lakes of Bosherston, Pembrokeshire, are covered with beautiful waterlilies.

Sea creatures

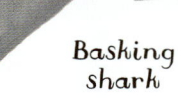

Basking shark

The basking shark is the largest animal in the waters around Wales.

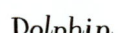

Dolphin

Dolphins and porpoises are seen in the waters around Wales, especially in Cardigan Bay.

Porpoise

Grey seals are mostly seen along the Pembrokeshire and Llŷn Peninsula coasts.

Areas of Outstanding Natural Beauty

There are five areas of outstanding natural beauty in Wales:
- Anglesey
- Llŷn Peninsula
- Gower Peninsula (the first in the UK, in 1956)
- Wye Valley
- Clwydian Range and Dee Valley

Half the world population of Manx shearwater birds breed on the islands of Skomer, Skokholm, Ramsey and Bardsey.

Teifi Marshes, Cardigan
A good place to see kingfishers and otters.

The Normans brought rabbits to Wales in the 11th and 12th centuries.

Some rare bats, such as the **Greater Horseshoe Bat**, live in Wales.

Hundreds of **red squirrels** live on Anglesey, the largest population in Wales. They can also be seen in the Clocaenog forest in Denbighshire, the forests of mid Wales and the upper Towy Valley.

Perhaps *beavers* will be reintroduced in Wales. They became extinct here in the 15th century.

Puffins
Puffins nest on Skomer Island, Pembrokeshire and other islands in west and north Wales.

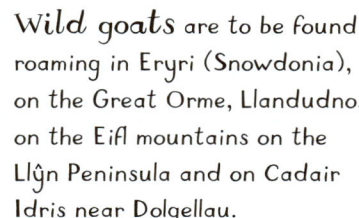

Deer
The red deer is the largest wild animal in Wales.

People say that many *big cats* are roaming wild in Wales.

Many *fallow deer* live in parks such as Margam (Port Talbot) and Dinefwr (Llandeilo).

Fallow Deer

Wild goats are to be found roaming in Eryri (Snowdonia), on the Great Orme, Llandudno, on the Eifl mountains on the Llŷn Peninsula and on Cadair Idris near Dolgellau.

Many conifer forests were grown in Wales in the 19th and 20th centuries to produce wood.

The **Llangernyw Yew** is the oldest tree in Wales. It is between 4,000 and 5,000 years old.

Farm animals

There are over a quarter of a million milking cows in Wales. Most are Friesians.
Welsh Black Cattle and White Dinefwr Park Cattle are special Welsh cattle breeds. The laws of Hywel Dda mention Welsh white cattle in the 9th century.

The Welsh Pig is white with lop-ears.

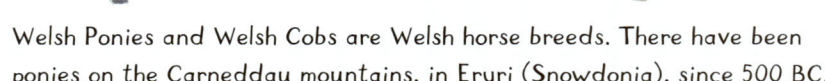

Welsh Ponies and Welsh Cobs are Welsh horse breeds. There have been ponies on the Carneddau mountains, in Eryri (Snowdonia), since 500 BC.

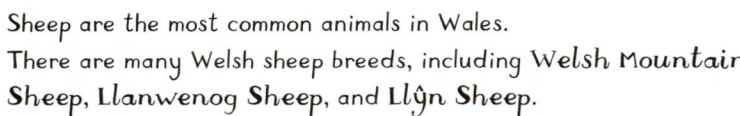

Sheep are the most common animals in Wales.
There are many Welsh sheep breeds, including **Welsh Mountain Sheep**, **Llanwenog Sheep**, and **Llŷn Sheep**.

Royal Welsh Agricultural Show
Farmers and visitors enjoy the Royal Welsh Show in Llanelwedd every July.
Local agricultural shows are held all over Wales.

FOOD

You can go to a **farmers' market** in your area to buy local produce.

Welsh cakes are a traditional and delicious treat made on a griddle. Welsh people have enjoyed eating them since the end of the 19th century.

The Welsh are well known for growing and eating **leeks**, in cawl and Glamorgan sausages.

Cheese is made in nearly all areas of Wales. What is your local cheese?

There are several small Welsh producers of **chocolates, sweets** and **biscuits**.

Glamorgan sausages don't contain any meat, but rather breadcrumbs, Caerphilly cheese and leeks.

Caerphilly cheese
Coalminers used to like to eat this famous white, crumbly cheese.

Welsh rarebit consists of melted cheese mixed with milk, butter or eggs, on toast.

Bara brith (or speckled bread) used to be baked on the same day as ordinary bread. Sugar, dried fruit and spices were added to the bread dough. Today it's a richer teatime cake.

Laverbread is special seaweed which has been washed, boiled and minced. Women used to do this in the 18th and 19th centuries on the Pembrokeshire, Anglesey and Gower coast. It is still produced on Gower today.

The **Conwy mussel beds** are around half a mile from the town of Conwy, in the river Conwy estuary.

People from the Penclawdd area have been gathering **cockles** from the beds on the Burry Inlet for centuries. This used to be women's work while the men worked as colliers underground.

Sea salt from Anglesey is exported to over 22 countries all over the world.

There are many Welsh companies producing bottled **water**.

Welsh Whiskey from Penderyn, near Hirwaun, is an award-winning distillery.

Italians came to south Wales at the end of the 19th century to open cafés. Italian cafés selling **ice cream** and **coffee** are still popular today.

There are many creameries in Wales making butter, cheese, cream and yoghurt from local **milk**.

To make **cawl** or **lobscouse**, pieces of meat are boiled with potatoes and other vegetables such as carrots and leeks.

Pembrokeshire early new potatoes are the first from Wales in the shops. This is because of the county's mild climate.

Welsh lamb and **Welsh beef** are well known throughout the world as tasty and healthy meats.

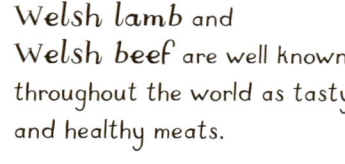

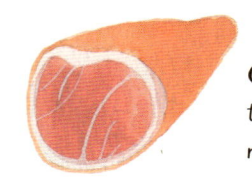

Carmarthen Ham is sold in the town's market and is used by many top chefs.

CARING FOR OUR COUNTRY

The Morlais Project off the coast of Holyhead is set to become the world's largest tidal stream energy site.'

There are three operational **wind farms** in North Wales – Gwynt y Môr, Rhyl Flats and North Hoyle.

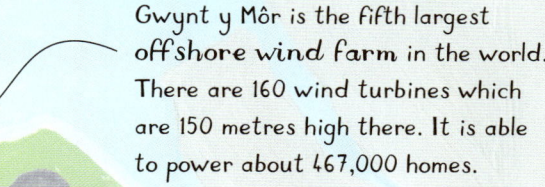

Gwynt y Môr is the fifth largest **offshore wind farm** in the world. There are 160 wind turbines which are 150 metres high there. It is able to power about 467,000 homes.

There are some large **solar farms** on Anglesey, and others are being planned.

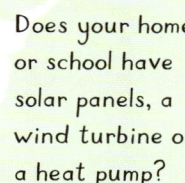

Does your home or school have solar panels, a wind turbine or a heat pump?

Wales has plenty of **water** resources. There is enough water in our reservoirs for the people of Wales and many areas in England too. But it's important that **we don't waste** water.

The **Centre for Alternative Technology** shows how we can live without destroying the earth.

Wales was one of the first countries in Britain to stop shops giving out free **plastic bags**, in 2011. It's important to stop plastic polluting our rivers, our lakes and our seas.

Wales has **Marine Protected Areas** to make sure that the seas are clean and the wildlife is healthy.

How can we stop waste and pollution?
Remember the 5 Rs:

· **Refuse** to buy products you don't need.

· **Reduce** waste by not buying products you will not use.

· **Reuse** by upcycling (using something in a different way).

· **Repair** broken items, rather than throwing them away.

· **Recycle** everything you can't reuse or repair.

Walking and cycling instead of travelling by car helps to stop pollution. Car sharing is also a good idea.

Electric cars are becoming more popular. They are much cleaner than diesel and petrol cars.

Wales's three **National Parks** help to protect the environment.

Many Welsh farms produce natural, **organic food**. They don't use insecticides which can poison the soil.

In Wales, we are trying to be **sustainable**. This means looking after the **resources** of Wales and the world.

If we buy locally-produced food, there is less **pollution** as it doesn't have to be transported far.

Is your school an **Eco-School**? The Eco-Schools initiative tries to inspire pupils to look after the environment. For example, by recycling, using less energy and switching off lights and appliances.

Solar panels are used to help to power Flat Holm, off the coast of Cardiff. They can be unrolled like a carpet from a trailer in two minutes.

LAND OF MY FATHERS

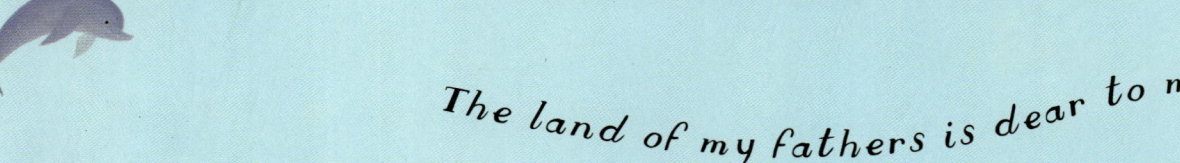
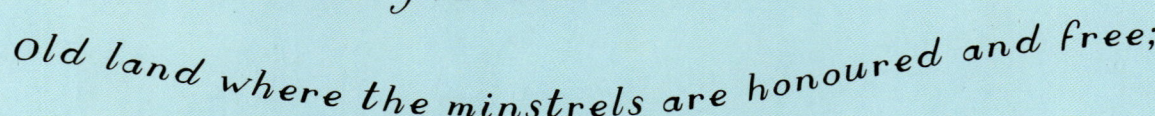

The land of my fathers is dear to me,

Old land where the minstrels are honoured and free;

Its warring defenders so gallant and brave,

For freedom their life's blood they gave.

Chorus: Land, land, true I am to my land,

While seas secure the land so pure,

O may the old language endure.

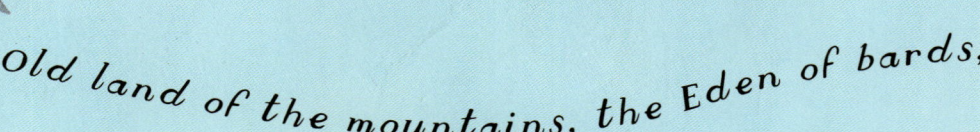

Old land of the mountains, the Eden of bards,

Each gorge and each valley a loveliness guards;

Through love of my country, charmed voices will be

Its streams and its rivers to me.

(Chorus)

Though foemen have trampled my land 'neath their feet,

The language of Cambria still knows no retreat;

The muse is not vanquished by traitor's fell hand,

Nor silenced the harp of my land.

(Chorus)

W. S. Gwynn Williams © Cwmni Cyhoeddi Gwynn